Disappearing Acts

Disappearing Acts
Gender, Power, and Relational Practice at Work

Joyce K. Fletcher

The MIT Press
Cambridge, Massachusetts
London, England

This book was set in Sabon by Achorn Graphic Services, Inc.

Printed and bound in the United States of America.

Library of Congress Cataloging-in-Publication Data

Fletcher, Joyce K.
  Disappearing acts: gender, power, and relational practice at work / Joyce K. Fletcher.
    p. cm.
  Includes bibliographical references and index.
  ISBN 0-262-06205-4 (hc.: alk. paper)
  1. Women engineers. 2. Corporate culture. 3. Women engineers—psychological aspects. 4. Sex roles in the work environment. 5. Organizational behavior. I. Title.
TA157.F54 1999
305.43′62—dc21   99-17937
                                                                          CIP

To Stephanie
who taught me about relational practice
and
Joseph
who taught me about voice

Contents

Preface

This is a book about relational work and the disappearing acts that render it invisible in today's workplace. It is written for the many people who find that the off-line, backstage, or collaborative work they do, and the relational skills this kind of work requires, are not recognized or rewarded at work. But that is only part of the story because, at its heart, this is a book about why this kind of work—what I call relational practice—is "women's work" and why that makes the story of its disappearance so much more interesting.

It owes much to the good nature and the intellectual and emotional support of others. First and foremost it owes an intellectual debt to the work of Jean Baker Miller. It is often said that all research is autobiographical, and if that is true, this book is a good example. In many ways, it is a book about my own journey in reclaiming and revaluing relational work, a journey that began many years ago when I first read her book *Toward a New Psychology of Women*. The ideas in that book energized me in a way few things have since. I am deeply grateful to her not only for her intellectual insight and determination to challenge the status quo by listening closely to women's experience and articulating it as knowledge but also for her willingness to communicate these revolutionary ideas simply, making them accessible to the likes of me, who, at the time, was a young, stay-at-home mother of three.

The study at the core of the book was driven by my desire to put to work what I learned from that book. The energy that drove the study's design was fueled by a desire to continue learning from women and a hunger to right injustice by adding what I thought was missing—feminine wisdom and experience—to organizational knowledge. It is interesting that only after the research was done did I find the work of Mary Parker Follett, someone who tried to add feminine wisdom and knowledge to organizations years ago.[1]

Indeed, many of the key features of relational practice described in this book were described by Follett in the early 1920s. While the similarities in the concepts are striking, the more interesting question is why Follett's work was invisible to me as a student of organizations. It was not invisible only to me. Peter Drucker notes that back in 1941, when he was thirsty for work on the process of management, he asked far and wide for lists of relevant work. No one mentioned Mary Parker Follett, despite her prominence a mere twenty years earlier. His explanation is that her ideas were ahead of their time.[2] Others, like Rosabeth Moss Kanter, reject this explanation and suggest that Follett's invisibility in organizational discourse is related to her gender. Kanter suggests that, like women who express ideas in meetings and are not taken seriously until someone else repeats them, Follett's work was not credited because of her gender.[3]

The story of disappearing acts suggests that neither of these reasons go to the heart of the matter. The reason is closer to what John Child suggests when he notes that "Elton Mayo's approach was seen at the time to be complementary to Follett's, yet soon came to eclipse it." Why? Because, he notes, Mayo's approach "ascribed a privileged rationality to managers that legitimated their authority and was naturally attractive to members of the management movement working on their behalf." This interpretation of the ideas was "intrinsically alien to Follett's basic premises."[4] In other words, the transformational aspect of Follett's ideas were lopped off and the principles were incorporated into the managerial discourse in weakened form, castrated and unable to challenge the status quo of organizational norms.

The study of relational practice offered in this book suggests that the disappearing acts that silenced Follett's work are alive and well in today's workplace. The main problem with this for organizations is not that these disappearing acts disappear women. The problem for organizations intent on transforming themselves to meet the challenges of the twenty-first century is that these disappearing acts disappear the feminine—and potentially transformational—aspects of new ideas. I hope men and women, managers and non-managers, organizational theorists and academics will find something of interest in reading about relational practice and the disappearing acts that render its challenge to organizational norms invisible. But the disappearing dynamic presents special challenges for women and for that reason the strategies to get beyond disappearing are written with women in mind.

A lot of invisible work has been invested in me, and this book, by family and friends. I am grateful for the support of my family—which has grown over the course of this work, to include not only my husband Bill, my daughters Pamela and Elizabeth, and my son Bill, but also a new son-in-law Bertrand, husband of Elizabeth. I am especially appreciative of my husband's faith in me and his determination to provide whatever type of support I needed, from notes of encouragement slipped into my work folders to plates of home-cooked lasagna served on our kitchen table in Maine amidst the litter of papers and a laptop computer. For his good humor, ability to empathize, and willingness to be used as a source of data—sharing his masculine experience and reactions to these ideas, sometimes freely, sometimes reluctantly, but sharing them nonetheless— I offer a heartfelt thank you.

I am especially grateful to Erica Foldy for calling attention to the need to highlight the action behind disappearing, with her suggestion that the book be called *Disappearing Acts*. The ideas in the book have so many intellectual parents it is hard to know where to begin. I am grateful to Deborah Kolb and Lotte Bailyn for their encouragement and contribution to these ideas during the original research project, and to those who engaged with the topic, willing to share their own experience and who in the sharing added greatly to the final product: Maureen Harvey, Susan Eaton, Judy Jordan, Irene Stiver, Roy Jacques, Meryl Reis Louis, Marion McCollom, Deborah Merrill-Sands, Marge Mulkerin, Christina Robb, Tim Hall, and Diane Cermak. Nancer Ballard, Pat Yancey Martin, Debra Meyerson, and Laura Woodburn offered suggestions on an earlier version of the manuscript that much improved its content as well as style. A special thank you goes to Lotte Bailyn and Jane Dutton who, in addition to providing encouragement, helpful input, and intellectual fodder, have demonstrated a belief in the value of the work that has helped me believe in it, too. I am grateful, too, to Rhona Rapoport, who pushed me to rethink the practical connection between gender equity and work and family issues, to Dave Brown, who introduced me to the notion of the unobtrusive exercise of power, and to June Zeitlin, who, as a representative of the Ford Foundation, supported the fieldwork for the study. Finally, I am grateful to the many women whose stories make up the tale of relational practice: the design engineers in the original study and the many women who have heard the story since and have added their own stories to it, taking the work beyond itself.

Disappearing Acts

Introduction
Being Invisible and Getting Disappeared

Consider these recent incidents in three of today's "new" organizations:

• In a major high-tech firm, a design engineer spends a good chunk of time with someone from another division, sharing some preliminary solutions to a design problem her team has been working on for the past six months. She leaves the meeting pleased that she has helped the company avoid reinventing the wheel. But later that night, as she ponders how she spent her day, she wonders if she has been foolish. Although she thinks she may have saved his team months of effort by responding to this engineer's request for a meeting, she worries that he is going to look far better than he should. Knowing the way things work, she worries that she and her team will get no credit for the help they gave him. Worse, they might even get eclipsed in the promotion of what she believes might be an innovative solution to one of the project's more persistent problems.

• At a scientific research center, a technical analyst suggests an obscure statistical methodology for a groundbreaking study. He works with the scientists to interpret and write up the results so the implications will be clear to those with less sophisticated statistical skills. The senior scientist is appreciative of his help and thanks him repeatedly. The technician is pleased because, often, his role is kept at a minimum, and he simply runs the program and troubleshoots. It is rewarding to know his ideas influenced the design of the study and the scope of the impact it was likely to have. But, later, as he listens to the research team present preliminary findings to visitors from another center, he realizes that thanks are always given verbally, either in private or as a footnote to the main presentation. He knows his contribution was critical to the project. It is nice to be thanked, but he wonders why he has never been asked to share the podium at internal events such as these or been listed as a contributing author.

• And, finally, in a mid-size manufacturing firm undergoing a reorganization to "self-managed teams," team members are discussing the criteria they will use to evaluate their performance. As they talk about critical core competencies, an analyst suggests that the ability to bring people together, to resolve differences, and make team members feel at ease with each other is something that is very important in getting a diverse group of people working well together. Although everyone agrees these competencies are important, they are not added to the list because, as another member notes, they are not measurable or something that could be written into one's objectives. The person who made the suggestion falls silent but later confides that she feels discouraged because the very thing that she feels is her most valuable contribution to the team—outweighing, in her opinion, even her technical capability—remains invisible as a competency.

What are we to make of these incidents? The engineer, technician, and analyst in these vignettes certainly seem to be in line with the requirements of today's organizations. Taking time from one's individual "deliverables" to share information with a coworker, adding one's statistical expertise to a groundbreaking research effort, and providing the less tangible competencies a team needs to work together effectively are all behaviors that fit the new emphasis on teamwork, collaboration, partnering, and learning. Organizations of the future, we are being told, will need to move from hierarchical systems of prediction and control to more team-based structures and reward systems. They need to be, in the words of General Electric's CEO Jack Welsh, "boundaryless,"[1] where information is shared freely and openly across divisions and functional barriers. These organizations will need a new kind of worker, one who is a continuous learner as well as a continuous teacher, who is willing to enable and empower others, to take responsibility for problems and work collaboratively with others to solve them. Moreover, we are told this new worker will need "multiple intelligences."[2] Rather than simply having technical skill, the worker of the future needs to be someone who can think creatively and who has what is often called "emotional intelligence," or the ability to work effectively with others, understanding the emotional contexts in which work gets done.[3] Certainly, the workers in the vignettes above seem to qualify. So why is it that they experience a sense of regret or failure in trying to work this way? Why is it that although there is an espoused organizational belief in collaboration and supportive teamwork, people who exhibit such behavior seem to *get disappeared*[4] from the organizational screen?

The study of female design engineers reported in this book suggests that answering these questions is complicated. Findings from the study indicate that the problem goes far beyond a simple disconnect between new requirements and antiquated performance appraisal systems. Instead, it has to do with issues of gender and power and the way certain behaviors "get disappeared"—not because they are ineffective but because they get associated with the feminine, relational, or so-called softer side of organizational practice. This implicit association with the feminine tends to code these behaviors as inappropriate to the workplace because they are out of line with some deeply held, gender-linked assumptions about good workers, exemplary behavior, and successful organizations. In other words, the findings suggest that there is a masculine logic of effectiveness operating in organizations that is accepted as so natural and right that it may seem odd to call it masculine. This logic of effectiveness suppresses or "disappears" behavior that is inconsistent with its basic premises, even when that behavior is in line with organizational goals. The result is that organizations adopt the rhetoric of change—moving, for example, to self-managed teams—but end up disappearing the very behavior that would make the change work, such as recognizing the effort involved in helping a team work together effectively. This book is about the gender-related dynamics that drive this disappearing process. It explores how the issues of gender, power, and the new organization collide and interact with each other and the paradoxical questions this raises for organizations and the people—especially the women—who work in them.

The Book

The study at the heart of this book was not designed to explore organizational transformation or the new organization per se. Instead, it started out as a theoretical treatise to explore—and challenge—the masculine bias in organizations from a feminist perspective. The intent was to bring together several different, somewhat disparate theoretical perspectives to examine the role gender plays in organizations as a systemic, rather than individual, characteristic. In designing the study I started from the premise that the current, commonsense definitions of work, success, and competence in organizations were not gender-neutral concepts, but rather, were definitions with a masculine bias. That is, they were definitions that implicitly valued certain (masculine) aspects of work and the people (mostly men) who tended to work this way, while making invisible other, arguably as important (feminine) aspects of work and devaluing the people (mostly women) who tended to work this way. The goal of the study was to give voice to these excluded aspects of work by detailing a way of working—relational practice—that was rooted in a relational or stereotypically feminine value system.

Although the goal was largely theoretical, the findings, particularly the discovery of how organizations might be "disappearing" the very behaviors they need to be successful, indicated that what had started out as a theoretical feminist treatise had some surprisingly practical implications for a broad range of organizational issues such as identifying critical competencies, changing corporate culture, and breaking the "glass ceiling."[5] The book will explore this unexpected linking of gender dynamics and organizational effectiveness. However, because it was designed with a different goal in mind, it will do so in a way that may feel strange to those who are used to reading more mainstream business research, such as case studies or the analyses of large samples of survey data. The study of relational practice is none of these. It is a postmodern qualitative study that uses nontraditional research methods and highly selected data to explore the social construction of gender in the workplace.

There are important reasons why the study was designed as it was and why it employed some nontraditional methods of inquiry and analysis. To help the reader understand these reasons, I adopt a feminist practice and begin the book with a chapter that offers a more personalized account of the research. The first chapter gives the story behind the study— its origins, the history of the passion and energy that drove its design; and the dilemmas, issues, and questions it was trying to answer. Chapter 1 describes not only how the study came to be, but how it came to be important to me.

Chapter 2 gives an overview of the three different research perspectives that form the study's theoretical foundation—feminist poststructuralism, a feminist sociology of work, and relational psychology. I like to think of the study as positioned at the intersection of these three bodies of work, focused on the areas of overlap but keeping in view those aspects that are contradictory and at odds with each other.

The first research perspective, feminist poststructuralism, deals with issues of power. It focuses on how meaning is constructed and how what we think of as commonsense definitions or natural, self-evident truths are actually reflections of dominant cultural assumptions. This perspective sets the stage for exploring why certain aspects of the feminine might be absent from conventional definitions of work. It asks, for example, Who is benefiting from the current definition? Whose interests are being served? What power relationships are being maintained and reinforced by current definitions? The second body of research, a feminist reading of the sociology of work, adds a slightly different perspective. It focuses on the specific definition of work in Western society and how that definition relies on gender distinctions and a dichotomous separation of domestic work from work in the public arena. This research perspective explores how gender is linked to what society considers *real* work. The last research perspective, relational psychology, is a body of work that explores women's psychological development. It is used to understand the term *feminine* as it is used in this study and identify what aspects of work this term might define.

Although chapter 2 contains some unavoidable academic jargon, I hope most readers, even those not used to academic vernacular, will give it a chance. I think it provides an important lens not only for interpreting the study but also for understanding its limitations.

Chapter 3 describes the research methods used and highlights the methodological issues and dilemmas I encountered in designing a study that bridges these three different research perspectives. The chapter positions the study as feminist poststructuralist fieldwork and gives the rationale for choosing an engineering firm and an all-female subject pool. It also explains how the data were collected—a combination of observation and interviewing techniques—and how they were analyzed. I like to think of this chapter as giving the reader a roadmap to help navigate the research terrain of the study, calling attention to what may be unfamiliar in the way the findings are reported. This is the chapter that will help readers understand why the findings are reported in two parts and why it was important to interpret the data through two different lenses each using different interpretive criteria.

Chapter 4 describes the first phase of the findings. It details four types of relational practice and gives examples of each type of activity, using direct quotes from the six engineers who were shadowed and interviewed.

Chapter 5 describes the second phase of the findings, those related to gender/power dynamics. It gives examples of the ways in which each of the four types of behavior were acted on by the larger organizational system. In other words, it gives an account of how relational practice was not just invisible, but was rendered invisible, or *disappeared,* by specific actions. These disappearing acts are described as a network of formal and informal practices, processes, and structures, as well as a set of common understandings and norms that make up the work culture of this particular organization.

Chapter 6 discusses the findings and their broader implications. While it includes a discussion of the implications for organizations, the primary focus of the chapter is on helping women understand the complicated gender dynamics that are at play in today's so-called new organization. Thus, the last chapter will emphasize strategies and techniques that individuals—particularly women—can use not only to enhance their own effectiveness and protect themselves from getting disappeared, but also to help their organizations be more effective.

1

The Story behind the Story

To understand the study and its nontraditional design and theoretical foundations, this chapter will give the personal history that lies behind the study. It will tell the story of how I came to be interested in these particular research questions and came to see certain types of information as the important data to gather in order to answer them. Telling the story behind the research is a common tradition in feminist research. In fact, conventional feminist wisdom holds that the story behind the story is crucial to understanding research because all research—feminist or otherwise—is value-laden and cannot escape being influenced by the history, life situation, and particular worldview of the researcher.

Of course, in most research reports we know very little about the researcher other than his or her institutional affiliation. Instead, we usually are asked to accept the notion that facts simply speak for themselves. But feminist research, perhaps because it so often taps into experience not represented in the mainstream, is more apt to acknowledge that facts cannot speak for themselves. It is more apt to adopt the perspective of those, such as Lotte Bailyn, who point out that research analysis and interpretation is a cognitive process, deeply personal and influenced by initial beliefs and outlook.[1] All research—the particular question it finds important to ask, the point of view from which the question is posed, the source of the data used to find answers, and, of course, the interpretation and conclusions drawn from the analysis—are surely, albeit invisibly, influenced by the standpoint of the researcher.[2]

The standpoint of the researcher can be a significant source of new knowledge. It is a lens that can help a researcher gather and understand data that might be invisible to others, adding a particular story and perspective to a body of knowledge that might otherwise be lost. In feminist tradition, acknowledging standpoint is important in another sense as well. It invites readers to join the interpretive process as partners. Researchers, no matter how comprehensive their studies are, can only hope to tell one part of the story, or one story among many others that could be told. When a researcher's standpoint is made explicit, it helps readers understand what particular story is being told and invites them to connect this story to other perspectives they hold. It is in this feminist tradition of invitation and joint inquiry that I offer the following account of how this research came to be and how it came to be important to me.

The research questions at the heart of the study came from an experience I had several years ago. As a full-time, stay-at-home mother of three young children, I read a book that had a powerful effect on me. This book, the first edition of Jean Baker Miller's *Toward a New Psychology of Women,* went to the heart of a conflict I was feeling between my career ambitions and my desire to retain a sense of connection and caring for others in my life. I read the book during a time when I was pondering my future, wondering whether I wanted to return to my profession as an elementary school teacher or go back to school to prepare for something less gender-typed. As a budding feminist—a charter member of *Ms.* magazine and ERA activist—I was determined to play a role outside the home. But I felt some ambivalence about what that role should be. The conclusion I drew from my feminist readings was that if I wanted to do something other than teaching, I would need to make some significant changes in who I was and what I valued. I spoke passionately about equality and about the need to dispel myths about women's nature and capabilities. I wanted to take my place in what I saw as the male world of power and influence, but, at the same time, there was a part of me that wondered, did I really want to be like the powerful men I saw around me?

The book offered a new way of thinking about things. Reading it gave me the courage to listen to my own voice and to question some of the masculine standards I was using to judge my life, my accomplishments, and my assessment of what I needed to do to develop myself and restart my career. What was new and exciting to me was the way Miller made visible, and then questioned, the masculine nature of some very basic human assumptions. She suggested that mainstream theories of human growth—ideas that had been developed by listening only to men's experience—did not fit women very well. Listening to and learning from women's experience, she offered something new, a relational theory of human growth and development that she and her colleagues later called *growth-in-connection*.[3] The central tenet of this theory is that growth is not so much a process of separating and individuating oneself from others, but something that occurs in a context of relational connection with and to other people. The book identified certain relational skills and attributes that are essential to this type of growth. In a departure from other books about women's voice, Miller suggested that this alternative model of growth-in-connection actually reveals important truths that are relevant not only to women's psychological growth but to all human development.

There were two specific ideas in the book that captured my attention. The first was that the relational traits I valued in myself and others, such as empathy, vulnerability, and connection, could be conceptualized as strengths rather than as weaknesses or emotional dependencies. Interpreting these attributes as skills that are essential to all human growth and development, instead of deficiencies that need to be overcome in order to make it in the "real" world, gave me a tremendous feeling of energy and hope. I started to think that maybe I could work toward gender equity in a different way. Perhaps I could pursue personal goals of competence and achievement in the world without giving up parts of myself that I valued. Indeed, and this was a radical thought for me at the time, perhaps the world needed more of this relational skill, not less.

The second idea I found compelling was the analysis of why relational attributes were not commonly seen as strengths but, instead, as feminine traits associated with women's greater emotional needs. Miller noted that because men are socialized to devalue and deny in themselves the relational skills needed to survive psychologically, they tend to rely on women to provide these attributes. Women, on the other hand are socialized to provide these skills, usually invisibly and without any acknowledgment that any need exists or anything valuable is being done. Thus, women become the "carriers" of relational strengths in society, responsible for creating relational connections for others and meeting basic relational needs without calling attention to the needs themselves. Rather than strengths, these relational attributes are commonly described as deficiencies (e.g., emotional dependency, weakness, vulnerability). This allows society to perpetuate the myth of self-reliance and independence, even though most people have a (largely female) network of people supporting their "individual" achievement.[4]

This notion of woman as a societal carrier of relational responsibility felt right to me. Not only did it fit my own experience but it gave me a new way of understanding the vehemence, resistance, and even violence that seemed to accompany women's move out of traditional roles. It helped explain why there seemed to be such different reactions to women and men who violated sex-stereotypes. Men were ridiculed and perhaps even shamed, but the sense of outrage and resistance seemed less pervasive than that shown toward women who defied stereotypes. Miller's analysis helped explain why. A man who exhibits more relational tendencies is not threatening to give up aspects of himself that others need to survive psychologically. His move out of sex-stereotyped behavior may be somewhat threatening, and there may be a line (homosexuality, for example) he must not cross. But a woman moving away from a relational stance represents a different kind of threat. If she should give up her responsibility for taking care of relational needs—whether at the individual, family, or even societal level—the psychological health and well-being of all these systems would be jeopardized. Her move away from relationality is, in a very real way, life-threatening.

The question that intrigued me was how society would handle this situation. What types of things would happen if women stopped providing relational opportunities for growth? If indeed this role was essential to human development, then it seemed to me that society could not afford to let women move from this role and adopt the masculine characteristics needed to survive in the world of power and influence. Or, at the very least, society, particularly powerful men who depended on women for support and encouragement, would not allow this to happen without a lot of anger and a strong sense of betrayal.

I wondered whether all the anger and frustration about child care and work/family issues that seemed to be directed at women were perhaps another manifestation of this same issue—anger and frustration because women should continue to take care of things (like providing the next generation of workers) invisibly, without calling attention to what they were doing. The backlash against women who aspired to positions of power and influence seemed to be cloaked in questions about what was best for society—Who was taking care of the children? What would happen to families?—but I wondered if the real threat might not be broader than that, something that threatened the way society took care of its relational needs. Resistance to women's changing roles was often seen, at least in the popular feminist essays I was reading, as resistance to sharing power. The image of women as "carriers," invisibly shouldering relational responsibility, suggested that the threat might be more complicated than that and run deeper. It seemed to me that we, as women, could never really understand the glass ceiling or the strength of the forces keeping it in place if we did not address this more complicated dynamic in some way. In the face of these issues, it seemed unlikely that simply agitating for equality based on a notion of fairness would lead to real change.

Pondering these questions forced me to begin thinking about gender— and gender equity and gender discrimination—in a new way. Rather than thinking about individual men and women or about the individual intentions or good will of people, I began to think of these things as societal-level, systemic issues. I started noticing how the world was organized as if achievement were an individual phenomenon and how relational and support activities, although essential, were commonly devalued. I began to think of this not just as an interesting phenomenon but as a *gendered* phenomenon, which was embedded in societal norms and had the effect of keeping woman in her place. But the biggest change in how I thought about these issues had to do with what I saw as the route to social change. I started to think that real change would never happen through the legislative process alone. Real change would require a change of heart and a discussion of these issues at a much deeper level than current discourse allowed.

My interest in applying these notions to organizations came years later. In my doctoral training in business school I found myself dissatisfied with what I was reading in the management literature about women in the workplace. Most of the early research on gender focused on equity and eliminating structural and attitudinal barriers that denied women access to what was seen as the male world of rationality, power, and influence.

The goal of this early research was to show that women were as capable as men. Not surprisingly, most of the research published in business journals showed that there were no differences between the capabilities of men and women. Studies that did find differences interpreted them as coming either from discriminatory practices in things such as developmental opportunities or from socialization deficiencies that could and should be corrected. Rosabeth Moss Kanter offered the most nuanced analysis of gender differences by suggesting that they were related not to gender but to power and were simply natural strategies to employ when one was in a one-down or token position.[5]

The self-help books for women gave the same message, and although I recognized some truth in them, I also found them troubling. The message in these books was that women have been inadequately socialized. While we are capable of being as rational, competitive, and assertive as men, our early training holds us back. What was troubling to me was that no one seemed to be questioning the male standard that was being applied. I wondered what Jean Baker Miller, or Carol Gilligan, would say about these books, and I felt sure that looking at organizations from a perspective in which women's "deficiencies" were redefined as strengths would offer new ways of thinking about organizations themselves. I decided that this was the research topic I wanted to pursue. I wanted to add a feminine perspective to organizational theory, one that would challenge masculine standards, not only to promote women within the current environment but to challenge the current environment itself.

At the time, this idea seemed revolutionary to me but as I began to read more widely in the field I discovered a number of articles and books on something called the "female advantage."[6] These books seemed to suggest that the relational traits, characteristics, and attributes socially ascribed to women—things such as caring, being involved, helping, building webs of connection rather than hierarchies, seeking consensus—might actually be good for business and that women had a lot to offer organizations. I also discovered that many feminists questioned this work and felt it was reinforcing gender stereotypes and inhibiting women's progress. Some believed it inappropriately universalized women, ignoring important differences among them. Others maintained that this focus co-opted women, encouraging them to use their skills in the service of a bureaucratic system that by its very nature (*man*agement) oppresses women.[7]

My own assessment of the female advantage literature was slightly different. I appreciated the way these books questioned masculine standards and reframed stereotypically feminine traits as something that qualified rather than disqualified women for management. But it felt as though something powerful was missing in this work. Reading more carefully, I realized it was missing the two ideas I had found most compelling in Miller's *Toward a New Psychology of Women*. First, the description of feminine traits failed to capture the most radical tenet of Miller's model of relational growth: the belief in the power of relational interactions to affect change through mutual engagement and co-influence. In other words, the female advantage theorists advocated feminine traits as useful to organizations but lost what was relational and potentially transformational about them. It was the model of growth underlying relational activity—a model rooted in mutuality and empowerment—that, to my way of thinking, had the power to transform organizations.

Eventually, I wrote an article called "Castrating the Female Advantage,"[8] which noted how this absence of mutuality severely limits the power of relational interactions. The article called attention to the important difference between encouraging relational interactions in the service of some preordained organizational goal—something Jennifer Pierce calls *strategic friendliness*[9]—and encouraging relational interactions as a source of new knowledge, where the outcome was unpredictable because it was the product of the interaction. It seemed to me that if relational attributes were encouraged in organizations only for the purpose of managing people to achieve preordained instrumental goals, the organization might benefit, but little would really change. On the other hand, if a model of mutual growth and influence were adopted, organizations might really be challenged because this model would empower people. New voices would be heard, new perspectives would influence decisions, and new ways of doing business might surface.

My conclusion was that although the female advantage approach appeared to be challenging masculine standards it was actually incorporating relational values into organizational thinking from an instrumental, masculine perspective. This would be unlikely to challenge the current systems of power and hierarchy in organizations but would, instead, simply give the hierarchy another tool for its tool bag. In contrast, I knew I wanted to do research that would challenge rather than reinforce the status quo. To make sure the study used a powerful (rather than a castrated) feminine voice to challenge organizational theory, I decided that relational theory and its concept of mutual growth-in-connection must be included. In the end, I used relational theory to define one of the key concepts in the study, something I called a *feminine logic of effectiveness.* The tenets of this theory, I believe, are what adds power and teeth to its feminist challenge. It gives a specific definition of what is meant by feminine, something that I found missing in a lot of gender research, particularly the female advantage work.

The failure to define what is meant by "feminine" is a problem I wanted to address in my research design because I saw it as a critically important issue in how the research might be used or, more important, misused. When not defined clearly, notions of the feminine tend to rely on stereotypical visions of women as morally superior, innately more caring, giving, or selfless than others. This can reinforce the view that it is women's natural role to clean up after others, emotionally as well as in other ways.[10] Relational theory addresses this issue by defining the feminine in much more concrete terms, not as a set of attributes but as a belief system about how growth and effectiveness occur. Using relational theory allowed me to use this definition of feminine to challenge stereotypically masculine theories of effectiveness that assume growth occurs through a process of separation and individuation. That is why this theory is so important to the study. It is one of the three research perspectives that form the study's theoretical framework. The description of the theory in chapter 2 highlights the aspects that differentiate it from other theories of human growth and development, giving it what I think of as its power—a feminine logic of effectiveness—to challenge the very assumptions and foundations on which organizations are built.

The desire to offer organizations a model of effectiveness rooted in mutuality and growth-in-connection continues to be the source of energy and passion that drives my work. The study was designed to incorporate this model so that the findings could challenge the masculine logic of effectiveness from this specific vantage point and definition of "feminine." Nonetheless, now that the study is completed and there are findings to be discussed, I worry that despite the design, these findings may be misinterpreted. I worry they may be used to reinforce the assumptions and stereotypes of women as morally superior that have typecast them as naturally suited for certain jobs and not others. That is why I have used two chapters to explain the origins of the study: this chapter, with its personal account of the centrality of relational theory to the research questions, and the next chapter, which gives a full account of the three theoretical perspectives linking gender, power, and the definition of work to this relational model of growth. I believe it is only from the perspective of this particular model of effectiveness that the research findings can be interpreted and understood as a feminine challenge to the status quo. It is what differentiates relational practice from other descriptions of so-called feminine skills, allowing it to challenge rather than reinforce organizational norms.

But I am getting ahead of the story. In my early thinking about these issues, I found there was something else troubling about the female advantage: It sidesteps the question of gender relations and power at work. The female advantage describes a certain set of behaviors and assumes that the sex of the actor is immaterial. It assumes that women and men behaving in the same way will experience the same reaction and consequences. This ignores the long history of power differences between the sexes and the effect this history might have on how "female advantage" behavior is interpreted or experienced in organizations. More specifically, it ignores the important societal context in which relational growth takes place. It does not take into account the powerful dynamic Jean Baker Miller describes of how women are relied on to be the carriers of relational responsibility in society but at the same time are devalued for taking on this role.

The problem in ignoring these dynamics was clear. Miller suggested that women, by virtue of their sex, are routinely expected to act relationally, to meet emotional needs intuitively, to support others' achievements, and to create conditions in which others can grow. These behaviors are very similar to those described in the female advantage. But the female advantage does not address how women might be expected to behave this way and not be rewarded for it, or how this work might be invisible to others. I suspected that the power dynamic operating in relation to these skills might be the most interesting part of the phenomenon. And I suspected that if this power dynamic were operating the way Jean Baker Miller suggested, the female advantage might never end up advantaging women.

I wanted to capture these power dynamics in my research. But to do so I needed a view of power that went beyond the typical textbook theories that defined power as "A getting B to do something s/he otherwise would not do." The system of power that I needed to understand had little to do with individual intention or personal authority but was, instead, a systemic characteristic. It had to do with understanding how it came to be that certain behaviors were characterized as feminine and culturally ascribed to females and others were characterized as masculine and culturally ascribed to males. It had to do with understanding the societal-level processes that created assumptions and beliefs that became so commonplace that they were rarely questioned. It had to do with understanding an exercise of power that was covert and unobtrusive, where people behaved in a certain way, not because they were forced by "A" to do so, but because it seemed like the right, or only reasonable, thing to do.

To understand this kind of power I began reading poststructuralist theory, a form of postmodern philosophy.[11] Poststructuralists focus on the unobtrusive, systemic exercise of power and how dominant groups determine meanings. It is considered a radical view of power because it asks, in the words of Steven Lukes, "Is it not the most insidious use of power [to have people] accept their role in the existing order of things either because they see or imagine no alternative to it or they see it as so natural and unchangeable they value it as divinely ordained and beneficial?"[12] It is a research perspective that calls attention to the power of conventional wisdom. Rather than accepting that certain truths are self-evident, it asks how these truths came to be self-evident. It asks interesting questions such as: Who is benefiting from this definition? Whose interests are being served? Whose interests are being silenced? How did it come to pass that this is commonly accepted as true? What would happen if we rejected this truth claim and substituted another? The goal of postmodern critique is to disrupt the status quo, particularly the power systems in the status quo, by raising questions such as these. Raising questions does not require huge data sets, it requires only that an alternative truth be identified. The number of people who experience this alternative truth is less important than the detail and texture of the alternative because that is where the challenge lies.

As I read more of this perspective I realized that it offered a way of incorporating many of the power dynamics that were of interest to me. In thinking about power and patriarchy, I had read a number of essays that seemed to focus on individual intentions and agency (e.g., women colluded in their own subordination because "the hand that rocks the cradle rules the world," or men dominated because they were threatened and did not want to give up power and privilege). I wanted to do a study that moved away from this individualistic framing of the situation and looked at more systemic issues. Poststructuralism was a useful perspective because it offered a way of thinking about power that focused not on the individual intentions of people, but on the system of common, everyday assumptions that create reality. The locus of power that poststructuralists emphasize is not in individuals but in systems of shared meaning that reinforce mainstream ideas and silence alternatives. This was important because it captured the way that all members within systems of power— the marginalized as well as the dominant—were actors and agents in maintaining and reinforcing the status quo. In terms of methodology, it helped me see that the voice of the marginalized group would be not only a source of an alternative reality, it would also be a source of data about what Lukes called the most insidious exercise of power: the unobtrusive exercise of power whereby the marginalized internalize, accept, and give voice to dominant thinking.

When I was writing the paper on castrating the female advantage, I began to appreciate just how powerful an unobtrusive exercise of power could be. In coming up with the title, I tried to find a word that would connote a loss of female power, or convey a loss of the essence of female-ness, but I could find no word that was comparable in strength and meaning to *castrate*. This helped me understand the complicated nature of the "silencing" dynamic I was proposing to study and the central role that language plays in that dynamic, particularly in determining what ideas can and cannot be expressed.

While certainly not mainstream in the management literature, there were a few examples of academics who had written critiques of the management field using this poststructuralist perspective on power. These critiques started from the same premise that I wanted to adopt, one that

asserted that organizations were gendered, privileging stereotypical masculine qualities and values and devaluing feminine. Although they were
not field-based work, these essays were useful because they modeled a
way of disrupting commonly accepted truths about management by offering a feminine alternative. For example, Dennis Mumby and Linda Putnam challenge the way emotion, a stereotypically feminine attribute, is
denigrated in theories of organizational decision making, while rationality, a stereotypically masculine attribute, is reified. They note the impossibility, indeed the irrationality, of ignoring the influence of emotion on
the decision-making process. They offer a model that integrates rather
than dichotomizes these two aspects of the decision-making process and
specifically includes the role emotion plays in making decisions. They go
on to note that this integrated model of the decision-making process not
only might be more effective but also more reflective of what is really
happening in organizations.[13]

In a similar type of essay, Joanne Martin and Kathy Knopoff call attention to the way Max Weber's bureaucratic principles value the masculine
and devalue the feminine side of many gendered dichotomies. In discussing how objectivity is reified and subjectivity denigrated in organizational norms, they too note the impossibility of understanding what
happens in organizations from a purely objective stance. They offer an
alternative model that incorporates rather than ignores subjectivity and
suggest that this model offers a more accurate picture of organizational
practice.[14]

What I found interesting and instructive about these two examples was
that they did not claim that their new models were a "women's way of
decision making" or a "women's view of objectivity." Rather, they called
attention to how stereotypically masculine definitions and assumptions
suppress certain aspects of organizational life, leading to unrealistically
narrow views of concepts such as leadership and decision making. Each
essay used stereotypically feminine attributes, such as emotion and subjectivity, to challenge organizational definitions and raise the question of
why attributes such as these were absent from these definitions. Essays
such as these helped me understand how poststructuralist concepts could
be used to open up a dialogue in which new questions are asked and new
visions of organizing might surface.

The research study[15] I designed reflects my sense of these issues and of what needs to be better understood about women and work. It starts from a desire to count women's experience in organizations as knowledge and explore how the larger context of power relations between the sexes might be influencing how that experience is perceived and internalized. I suspect that at its heart is a desire to continue—and perhaps invite others to join—the journey of questioning masculine standards and envisioning alternatives that began for me with the reading of Jean Baker Miller's book. In an autobiographical sense, its design reflects an effort to understand what is behind the ambivalence, contradictions, and dilemmas I have felt as a woman who cares about achievement and personal excellence and who also cares about caring, connection, and community. It is a study designed to connect rather than divide, to unearth frameworks of understanding rather than assign blame or guilt. And it reflects my hope that deeper understandings of these issues can open up possibilities and leverage points for change, even in large social systems that seem impervious to change.

I drew on three different theoretical perspectives to create a framework that would hold all the aspects of the study that were important to me. Key concepts and specific definitions of words such as power, feminine, masculine, or the term *real work* are pulled from these three research domains. Each adds a perspective that is important in understanding the research questions and what types of conclusions can be drawn from the findings. The first domain is feminist poststructuralism. This perspective, with its emphasis on the relationship between knowledge, discourse, and power establishes the context of the study and positions it as a challenge to commonly held definitions of work. The second is a feminist reading of the sociology of work. It adds a way of understanding how conventional definitions of work are gendered because they reflect a splitting of the public and private domains of life along gender lines. The third perspective, relational psychology, suggests what might be missing or invisible in these conventional definitions of work. Each of these research perspectives, as well as a description of how they inform and interact with each other to create a theoretical foundation for the study, are described in the next chapter.

2

Theoretical Context

Feminist Poststructuralism

The concept of power I used in the study comes from a form of postmodern philosophy known as poststructuralist critique. This perspective calls attention to the way knowledge is produced and to the relationship between knowledge, power, and discourse.[1] It focuses on how some voices in the discourse are heard and counted as knowledge, while others are silenced, marginalized, or excluded. Poststructuralist critique gives voice to these marginalized perspectives and calls attention to the systems of power that have marginalized them. Feminist poststructuralism adopts these same principles but with a focus on the gendered nature of knowledge production and the way it maintains and reinforces the power relationships between the sexes. Thus, the goal of feminist poststructuralist inquiry is to add a specific marginalized voice to organizational discourse—women's voice—and, by doing so, disrupt a particular system of power: patriarchy.

While poststructuralist inquiry has many distinguishing characteristics, the most relevant to this study are (1) its perspective on the relationship between power and knowledge, (2) its emphasis on the role of language and other forms of representation in constructing experience, and (3) its concept of resistance.

Power-Knowledge
Poststructuralist inquiry calls attention to the relationship between power and knowledge and considers this relationship a central object of study. Unlike other research perspectives that assume facts speak for themselves,

poststructuralist perspectives see the production of knowledge as an *exercise of power* where only some voices are heard and only some experience is counted as knowledge. Poststructuralists challenge the notion of transcendent or universal truth and assert that the set of rules used to determine if something is true or false is not value free but is, instead, ideologically determined. Using these rules is an exercise of power because it maintains the status quo and silences any serious challenges to it. This relationship between knowledge and power is a key element of poststructuralist thought because it suggests that dominant ideologies maintain their dominance by simultaneously embracing the notion of transcendent truth and defining the rules that determine that truth. The process of producing knowledge is an exercise of power that is especially potent because it is not open to question: What is "true" is so consistent with the dominant ideology that it is supported by notions of common sense, nature, and divinely inspired order.

The goal of poststructuralist inquiry is to disrupt the relationship between power and knowledge by bringing what are called "subversive stories" into the discourse. Subversive stories usually take the form of personal accounts of members of a marginalized group whose voice has been silenced and whose experience has not been counted as knowledge. These stories disrupt the discourse by offering an alternative, often contradictory version of reality.[2] The power of adding a marginalized voice to the discourse is that it forces a recognition of the arbitrary nature of what is considered true. The goal is to offer the dominant group an opportunity to question these truths, or at least to consider that they are not universal.

Language and the Social Construction of Experience
Another key feature of poststructuralist inquiry is its emphasis on the role language and other forms of representation play in mediating the relationship between power and knowledge. It is a perspective that considers social reality—and its pattern of dominance—not as a given, but as something that is socially created through the process of representing experience. From a poststructuralist perspective there *is* no experience, there is no "knowing" self except that which is an effect of what is called "discursive practice."[3] In discursive practice, subjects and subject posi-

tions are created through a process of signification in which they are "named," such as consumer, preschooler, employee, etc. This naming invokes a relationship to societal practices and structures, which subjects then enact. In this way, a representation of experience is as much a *construction* of reality as it is a *reflection* of reality.

For example, poststructuralists note that signifiers such as "woman," "man," "mother," or "father" are subject positions that derive meaning not from something intrinsic but from the way ideology constructs them through language, material practices, and structural relationships. Thus, language not only reflects a certain reality, it also actively creates that reality and sustains the power relationships that depend on it. From a poststructuralist perspective, then, textual and material representation are never neutral but are instead powerful means of constructing an ideological worldview that furthers the interest of some dominant group.

Resistance

Resistance, the third key feature of poststructuralism, refers to the process of disrupting, or resisting, the unobtrusive exercise of power that occurs in the process of representing experience. The exercise of power in the representation process is not cast as absolute but as Stewart Clegg notes, is considered "contingent, provisional, achieved, not given."[4] Therefore, it can be resisted using destabilizing strategies that disrupt the discourse. For text, the most common destabilizing strategy is deconstruction. Deconstruction is the process of taking apart the text and analyzing it to challenge implicit dichotomies, reveal suppressed contradictions, and call attention to what has been obscured or made invisible. It is a powerful tool for challenging the assumptions that lie beneath the text. For example, challenging dichotomies means unpacking the ways in which these dichotomies (e.g., public/private, rational/emotional, mind/body) create meaning by implicitly devaluing one side of a linguistic pair and valuing the other. Calling attention to the valuation process makes it visible and opens up room for discussion and examination. It allows us to question assumptions that are rarely noticed. It prompts us to ask questions such as: Why is it that the rational is more highly valued in organizational decision making than the emotional?

Deconstruction also calls attention to what is not said and suggests that the suppressed in text operates like the unconscious in psychoanalysis—it is all the more powerful because it is invisible. The process of destabilizing text relies on the fact that just as the *construction* of text is a way of creating social reality, *deconstructing* the text is a way of disrupting this reality to reveal it as just one of many possible constructions. This creates an occasion to question and examine the role the original construction plays in maintaining current power relationships and to ask, for example, Who benefits from this construction of reality? Whose interests are being served?

Whatever method is used, this type of inquiry is not intended to replace one social reality with another or to claim one truth is preferable over another. After all, any text, even deconstructed text, can itself be deconstructed to reveal its underlying assumptions and biases. Rather than seeking a higher truth, this method of inquiry seeks to expand the dialogue to allow previously uncontested ideas, assumptions, and perspectives to be challenged. The goal is to create what poststructuralists call "discursive space," where dominant meanings can be *resisted*. Creating discursive space means dislodging the preeminence of those dominant meanings long enough to create, at least theoretically, a place where new things can be said and new social structures envisioned[5].

These three features of poststructuralist inquiry[5] outline the research terrain of the study. Putting the goals of the study in the language of this perspective it could be described as a study to destabilize the definition of work in organizational discourse by telling a feminist subversive story. The goal was to call attention to the masculine nature of the knowledge production processes that create commonly accepted definitions of organizational concepts such as work, competence, and skill. I planned to do this by discovering and giving voice to a feminine alternative that poststructuralist critiques suggested had been silenced or obscured. If found, I planned to add this voice to the discourse, thereby momentarily relaxing taken-for-granted assumptions about the nature of work. And finally, by relaxing these assumptions, I expected to be able to create discursive space in which new, less masculine ways of thinking about work, competence, and skill might be considered.

Feminist Sociology of Work

Definition of Work

In organizational discourse, the "truth rules" that determine the definition of work are derived from assumptions (i.e., a certain ideology) about the demands and goals of organizations. The clearest expression of this ideology can be found in the structural elements of organizing, articulated by Frederick Taylor as the tenets of scientific management and reinforced by Max Weber as the tenets of bureaucracy.[6] These include:

• a rational division of labor so that different people are assigned different jobs with fixed duties based on expertise, skill, and experience;
• a hierarchy of control and chain of command;
• a consistent set of abstract rules and procedures to ensure uniform practice and performance standards;
• a process of recruitment and advancement based on technical competence; and
• a standard method of record keeping and communication.

This emphasis on regimenting and rationalizing organizational life to make it predictable and supportive of an authority structure is the historical context in which the organizational discourse on work has evolved. Indeed, it is so ingrained that any suggestion of an alternative is likely to be met with the response, "But that's just the way organizations *are*." Thus, although there have been many challenges to these Weberian bureaucratic principles—and theories of organizing have been modified and amended in response to them—the basic elements continue to reflect the values of the Enlightenment and its emphasis on rationality and individuality. Examples of how organizational theory has reified these values of abstraction, linearity, control, and predictability abound. Management schemas such as Management by Objectives focus on breaking down jobs into a series of specific, concrete, measurable, and verifiable goals to be achieved in a specified time frame. Linear models of decision making[7] emphasize decision rules and problem attributes. Models of leadership and responsibility emphasize individual charisma and long-term, abstract thinking. Appraisal systems use the time span of responsibility to assess the importance of one's job to the organization by distinguishing high-level thinkers from low-level doers.[8] In the same vein, quantitative data intended to predict behavior are regarded as more valuable and reliable than qualitative data intended to contextualize it.[9]

In recent years, feminists have begun to call attention to the way these organizational values are closely aligned with images and attributes that have been socially ascribed to males. These images are deeply embedded in organizational life and are resistant to change.[10] Even when theories such as the garbage can theory of decision making[11] or the theory of bounded rationality[12] challenge the universal nature of these norms by suggesting that they do not tell the whole story or capture the total picture of organizational phenomena, they do little to challenge their preeminence.

From a poststructuralist perspective, the interesting question is: How did it happen that this particular view of desirable traits, values, and attributes came to be regarded as so normal that it is rarely challenged? Or, to be more specific and pose the question from a feminist perspective, How did it happen that these masculine values of abstraction, rationality, and control dominate organizational life, and what systems of power between the sexes do these masculine norms keep in place?

Public and Private Spheres

Feminists such as Sandra Harding suggest that the privileging of these qualities over others rests on the unquestioned acceptance in Western thought of certain gendered dualities, such as mind vs. body, reason vs. emotion, and objectivity vs. subjectivity. She notes that these dualities are reflective of a more general gender dichotomy between culture and nature, where men and masculinity are strongly associated with the public, cultural role and women and femininity with the private, natural role. This dichotomy divides the world into two separate, gendered domains— a public work sphere, where the dominant actor is assumed to be male, and a private family sphere, where the dominant actor is assumed to be female.[13] Although this public vs. private dichotomy is so pervasive as to seem inevitable many have pointed out that it is neither natural nor inevitable. Economists, sociologists, feminists, and, most recently, poststructuralist feminists all have offered explanations of the origins of this dichotomy. These differing explanations suggest that this dichotomy is in fact a social construction—one particular outcome among many possible.

Economic explanations of the division of public and private are rooted in Marxism and the rules of the marketplace, claiming that this split is a product of the Industrial Revolution. The logic is that as people were forced by the demands of industrialization and capitalism to move from being independent producers to selling their labor for wages, it became necessary to develop methods of control, specialization, and standardization to ensure organizational efficiency and guarantee a docile labor force. The principles we have come to accept as the foundation of organizational theory, such as Max Weber's tenets of bureaucracy, were developed in response to this need to systematize organizational life and control the labor force. As work became centralized in urban centers, routinized in shops and factories, and mechanized for efficiency, kinship groups were disrupted and more demands were placed on the family to meet industrial workers' unmet needs for autonomy, nurturing, and emotional sustenance—the expressive, supportive side of life. Workers came to see home as a refuge and a haven from the dehumanization of the workplace. Thus, each domain became increasingly specialized, meeting distinct societal needs and calling forth certain behaviors in its members. This explanation of the public/private split conceptualizes the two spheres as complementary—separate but equal domains that function together for the good of society.[14]

Feminists, however, take exception to this gender-neutral position and note that the notion of separate spheres actually reinforced a preexisting, patriarchal, gendered division of labor that fits neatly with the goals of capitalism.[15] That is, feminists argue that rather than explaining the public/private split, the demands of industrialization simply took advantage of a preexisting split and provided an economic rationale for its existence. Thus, woman's close association with nature, arising from the demands of pregnancy, childbirth, and child care made it convenient to assign her the role of providing a respite from the public arena in which capital goods were produced. This arrangement had several benefits for capitalist production. It created a consuming entity, the family, to ensure a market for the goods and services produced, and it established the family as the means of reproducing and socializing a continuing source of labor. It also established the notion of family wage, thus reifying the idea that woman's place was in the home. This had the effect of ensuring a cheap secondary labor force of women and children who would tolerate low wages and the vagaries of the market, being hired and fired in response to market demands.

This feminist understanding of the separation of consumption and production has several important implications for the definition of "real" work. The first has to do with affect and motivation. Work in the public arena, that is, activities associated with production, came to be seen as something one does out of obligation, and activities in the private arena were seen as something one does out of devotion. This distinction gave rise to the cult of true womanhood, the idealized image of woman as filled with loving devotion to her family, engaged in unselfish acts of self-sacrifice.[16] This notion of private-sphere activities as being motivated by love—a pure, idealistic motivation quite distinct from the motivation for money—tended to obscure the work involved in consumption and reproduction processes. It is love, not labor, that is salient in the labor of love women were expected to provide for their families. Thus the work (providing, nurturing, sustaining, and reproducing) and the unique skill and intelligence it required, disappear from the definition of "real" work because it is constructed as occurring naturally, motivated more by affection and emotionality than by intention and rationality.[17]

In summary, it is clear that there are a number of forces contributing to the creation and continuation of the public/private dichotomy. Many have noted that this dichotomy depends on an ideology of femininity and motherhood to sustain itself. For this discussion it is also important to note the obvious—that this dichotomy also depends on an idealized vision of manhood, one that does not fit the experience of many men. Thus, the public half of the public/private split is not only male gendered in a static sense, it also represents a privileging of instrumental processes that continually recreate and reinforce this image. The important point for this discussion is that the social construction of this dichotomy along idealized gender lines has led to a certain way of seeing and representing work in each sphere. The result is a certain set of characteristics associated with the subject position "worker" that is male gendered in the pub-

Table 1
Public and Private Spheres

Public Sphere	Private Sphere
Work is something you have to do	Work is something you want to do
Money is the motivator	Love is the motivator
Work is paid	Work is unpaid
Rationality reified	Emotionality reified
Abstract	Concrete, situated
Time span defined	Time span ambiguous
Output: marketable goods, services, money	Output: people, social relations, creation of community, attitudes, values, management of tension
Context of differential reward leads to focus on individuality	Context of creating a collective leads to focus on community
Skills needed are taught; work is considered complex	Skills needed are thought to be innate; work is considered not complex

lic sphere and female gendered in the private sphere. Table 1 summarizes these characteristics.

From a poststructuralist perspective, the problem with the separation of the two spheres is that it is a social construction: Although subject positions operate in both spheres, often simultaneously, the discourse (social practice, structures, and language) continues to create, reinforce, and textually represent them as separate and dichotomous.[18] This sets up a situation in which knowledge from one sphere is likely to be considered inappropriate to the other and thus unlikely to challenge its underlying narrative. As a result, public-sphere attributes such as rationality, cognitive complexity, and abstract thinking, are often absent from traditional definitions of work in the private, family sphere. By the same token, private-sphere attributes, such as emotionality, caring, and community, are often invisible in traditional definitions of work and competence in the public sphere.[19]

The situation is compounded by the fact that the two spheres are not only separate but are also gendered. That is, men and masculinity are normatively associated with the public, cultural role and women and femininity with the private, natural role. The result is a gender split in which the notion of growth, effectiveness, and an exemplary worker in the public work sphere is conflated with idealized masculinity, and in the private sphere, these same notions are conflated with idealized femininity. This suggests that assumptions about what is appropriate and inappropriate in each sphere are held in place not only by notions of separation, but also, and perhaps more firmly, by deeply held images of masculinity and femininity that function to keep patriarchal systems of power in place.[20]

Placing this discussion of the public/private spheres within a poststructuralist framework highlights several important features of the study. It suggests not only that the feminine is likely to be absent from organizational definitions of work, but also hints at a powerful process of representation in which aspects of work that are congruent with idealized masculinity will be considered "real" work and those that are associated with idealized femininity will not. It also suggests a strategy of resistance. Giving voice to feminine knowledge from the private sphere has the potential to disrupt and destabilize the gender/power dynamic inherent in the current definition of work and create discursive space in which new, less patriarchal definitions might emerge.

This strategy of resistance, however, raises two important theoretical issues. The first is, what "voice" can be used to bring feminine knowledge into organizational discourse? And the second is, how can this voice be brought into the discourse in a way that will preserve rather than co-opt its challenge to dominant meanings? Relational psychology offers a feminine theory of growth and effectiveness—relational theory—that provides the theoretical framework to address these issues.

Relational Psychology

First proposed by Jean Baker Miller and psychologists and psychiatrists at the Stone Center at Wellesley College and supported by the work of Carol Gilligan and others, relational theory and its correlates were developed by listening for and to the experience of women. Although it draws on Nancy Chodorow's extension of object relations theory and gender differences in early life experience, it makes no claim to speak for all women nor to claim that only women subscribe to it.[21] Nonetheless, it is a theory that positions itself as an alternative to the masculine bias in mainstream theories of psychological, intellectual, and moral growth that underlie many societal structures.

Relational theory suggests that although the prevailing models of adult growth and achievement are based on public-sphere characteristics such as separation, individuation, and independence, there exists an alternative model, called growth-in-connection, that is rooted in private-sphere characteristics of connection, interdependence, and collectivity.[22] Unlike mainstream models that emphasize autonomy and the individuation process as central to personal growth and identity[23] growth-in-connection models emphasize the role of relational interactions in the development process. While both mainstream and relational theories of growth encompass both individual and relational processes, it is the *preeminence* of connection and mutuality over individuation in the developmental process that marks relational theory as feminine and gives it the potential to challenge organizational discourse.

The basic tenet of relational theory, that growth and development require a context of connection, is further delineated by the identification of specific characteristics of growth-fostering connections. In other words, growth is conceptualized as occurring not in *any* engagement or relationship but through a specific kind of relational interaction. Growth-fostering interactions are characterized by mutual empathy and mutual empowerment, where both parties recognize vulnerability as part of the human condition, approach the interaction expecting to grow from it, and feel a responsibility to contribute to the growth of the other. The ability to develop relationally requires certain strengths: empathy, vulnerability, the ability to experience and express emotion, the ability to participate in the development of another, and an expectation that relational interactions can yield mutual growth. As Miller notes, however, the characterization of these attributes as strengths is itself a challenge to the dominant discourse, especially the psychological discourse in which giving preeminence to connection has traditionally been characterized as a weakness or psychological deficiency.

Although, as noted above, this model of growth does not presume to speak for all women, it does assert that there are strong forces operating to encourage women to enact it. These include internal forces based on early development and external forces based on socialization and societal expectations of gender-appropriate behavior.[24] Indeed, Jean Baker Miller, in the first edition of *Toward a New Psychology of Women,* offers a radical view of these societal expectations, proposing that because men are socialized to deny in themselves the relational skills needed to survive psychologically, they rely on women to be the carriers of these skills in society. Thus, society assigns relational activity to women and views it as "women's work." This suggests that enacting a relational model of growth is likely to be a site for the social construction of gender in the workplace, because it is behavior that marks one as "feminine."

Although many feminist research perspectives rely on notions of connection, Stone Center relational theory is distinct in three ways that make it particularly appropriate for the study of organizations. First, the Center's model delineates specific characteristics of growth-fostering interactions. These interactions form the substance of a relationship over time. However, delineating them at the level of a single interaction allows for a more sophisticated analysis than would broader relational concepts such as trust or safety. It creates, for example, the possibility of examining the growth-fostering nature of interactions between people who are connected on a sporadic or short-term basis, a common situation in work settings.

Second, the Stone Center model identifies specific criteria to determine if growth has occurred. It identifies the conditions necessary to achieve growth-in-connection and the five positive outcomes associated with that growth. Jean Baker Miller and Irene Stiver call these outcomes the "five good things." They include zest, empowered action, increased self-esteem, new knowledge, and a desire for more connection.[25] The distinguishing feature of these conditions and outcomes is *mutuality:* It is the presence of mutuality—in each of the conditions and in each of the outcomes—that determines if an interaction is or is not growth-fostering. In other words, it is not enough that one party in an interaction feel empowered or experience a desire for more connection. If the five outcomes do not accrue to both parties, the standard has not been met. This baseline presence of mutuality distinguishes the Center's theory of growth-in-connection from other feminine conceptualizations of connection and is the source of its challenge to organizational norms. It is a theory of "power with" that is a direct challenge to the theory of "power over" that underlies organizational principles of hierarchy.[26]

Third, the Center's model calls attention to the gender/power dynamic inherent in concepts of connection. It posits that growth-fostering connection is not a gender- or power-neutral concept. Through socialization processes, women are encouraged to accept the responsibility for relational growth and men are encouraged to deny it. This not only identifies relational interactions as a site for the social construction of gender, it identifies another process of social construction that is particularly relevant to organizations. That is, relational theory suggests that shouldering the obligation to create relational conditions for growth is done invisibly, without acknowledging either the support or the need for it. This allows the belief in independence and individual achievement to go unchallenged. In this way, relational theory offers a direct challenge to key organizational structures and principles based on the reification of individual achievement. It also calls attention to the way society in general and organizations in particular use female socialization as a free resource, simultaneously requiring and devaluing support activities. The result is a gender-segregated workplace that appears to be the result of natural selection rather than an exercise of power.

This discussion of the principles and distinguishing characteristics of relational theory provides the theoretical rationale for using it as a surrogate for a feminist ideology of effectiveness. Relational theory derives:

• legitimacy as feminine through its emphasis on connection rather than separation as the route to growth;
• legitimacy as a theory of effectiveness because it posits growth (the "five good things") as the motivation for and the outcome of relational interactions;
• legitimacy as feminist ideology because its tenets (mutuality, "power with," and the claim that individual achievement is a myth) embody direct challenges to the ideology underlying organizational systems of power and therefore give it the potential to disrupt organizational discourse.

The inquiry was designed as a field study, rather than the more common poststructuralist technique of textual critique, for several reasons. First, I wanted to challenge the organizational definition of work at the level of concrete, everyday work practice, rather than the more general level of work as depicted in written documents such as job descriptions, personnel manuals, or performance appraisals. Second, I was curious as to whether there were organizational actors already operating out of an alternative model of growth and effectiveness similar to the one underlying relational theory. By understanding their motivation in enacting this way of working, I hoped to be able to expand the theory and give additional examples of behavior that is characteristic of a relational belief system. At that time, most examples of practice enacting a relational model of growth and effectiveness had been gleaned by observing interactions in intimate relationships such as those between mother and child; among family members;[27] or in work relationships characterized by caring, such as nurse/patient or therapist/client.[28] Third, I wanted to see if I could capture any elements of the experience of socially constructing feminine gender in the workplace that might be related to enacting relational practice.

The first step in the plan was to collect a potentially destabilizing representation of work in an organizational setting. The ideal setting would gain its legitimacy from the extent to which it was an exemplar of public-sphere characteristics and their underlying logic of growth and effectiveness. The ideal subject would be someone who stood at what Dorothy Smith calls the "line of fault" between the public and private spheres. That is, someone who was located in two particular and inherently contradictory subject positions in organizational discourse—"woman" and "worker"—and who would embody the contradictory expectations and predispositions attending these two subject positions. The second step in the plan was to analyze the representation of work gathered from these subjects to reveal those practices that were motivated by tenets underlying relational theory. The third step in the plan was to compare this alternative reality to the mainstream definition of work in that particular organizational culture. I hypothesized that this comparison would highlight the differences between the two and reveal the mechanisms by which the alternative representation of work had been suppressed. The last step was to use the discursive space created by disrupting the conventional definition of work to envision new definitions.

The research questions guiding the inquiry are listed below:

1. Is there evidence that relational practice exists in this organizational setting? If so, what behaviors characterize it? What beliefs, assumptions, and values do these behaviors reflect?

2. What are the mechanisms through which relational practice and the belief system underlying it are brought into the dominant discourse and subjected to the "truth rules" of that discourse?

3

Methodology

Research Design

This study was an independent part of a larger action research project funded by the Ford Foundation. The overall project, which focused on issues of work, family, and gender equity, was conducted over a period of four years in a major high-technology company based in the northeastern United States. At the time the data in this portion of the study were collected, the research team had been on site for two years, engaged in a process of cultural diagnosis that involved interviewing people at all levels of the organization, shadowing key employees, attending a wide range of technical and staff meetings, and analyzing company documents and policy statements.[1] The relational practice portion of the study was conducted as an independent piece of the overall project. It was proposed and agreed to by the company in a discussion held after the findings from our diagnosis of the organization's culture had been presented to management. The stated goal of the study was to explore alternative ways of working by observing people who did not fit the "ideal worker" stereotype identified in the cultural diagnosis.

That this project was part of a larger, ongoing inquiry influenced the research design in some important ways. As a researcher in the larger project, I was a known commodity and had been afforded some degree of insider status. This facilitated the process and allowed for a design that in other circumstances might have been unworkable. It also allowed for a secondary set of data about the organizational culture in this setting that was not a formal part of this particular inquiry but was collected and analyzed in a manner consistent with it. Finally, participants in the study had been "trained" in a data collection methodology that was exploratory, characterized by observation, focus groups, and interviews with open-ended questions.

The research design and process used in this portion of the study are explained in two sections. The first provides an overview intended to give a sense of the theoretical and methodological factors that influenced the selection of data-gathering techniques. The second is a section on the research process, which reports the data collection and analysis procedure, including some unexpected complications that influenced how the procedures were conducted in the field.

Overview

As Gareth Morgan notes, the selection of a research method is more a theoretical than a methodological issue in that method reveals the researcher's particular theory of knowledge.[2] For this study, the theoretical perspective outlined in the previous chapter required a method that would bridge three different theoretical domains—poststructuralism, feminist sociology, and relational psychology—and two different, and to some degree contradictory, research design perspectives: feminist standpoint research and poststructuralist critique.

Feminist standpoint, or what is more commonly called *women's voice* research, is based on traditional qualitative research techniques typical of the interpretive research paradigm. This research strategy relies on data collection in real-life settings in which the researcher has no control over events, interactions, or situations. The design typically includes universalizing a group along at least one dimension (e.g., class, role, sex, race, etc.) thought to separate it from a dominant group and analyzing data about this marginalized group as a collective, seeking to find commonalities that constitute "one voice." In this way, standpoint research methodology rests on the same key theoretical assumption that underlies all ethnographic inquiry, namely that it is possible to infer a general belief system by observing patterns of behavior and listening closely to how subjects explain or make sense of their actions.[3]

Although standpoint research is rooted in this general tradition, it differs from other qualitative approaches by being intrinsically sensitive to issues of power. That is, one goal of standpoint research is to generate knowledge from a marginalized group's experience in order to add it to a general body of knowledge from which it is absent. Thus, this research position accepts as a given not only that groups have a distinguishable experience that exists but also that this experience has not been listened to or valued. The goal of the research is to explicate this experience and then add it, in a fairly straightforward manner, to previous conceptions.

In contrast, the goal of postmodern philosophy is critique. The intention is to call into question the underlying systems of thought that constrain, determine, or otherwise socially construct subjective experience. One of the key assumptions underlying poststructuralist critique is that there *is* no subjective reality independent of the socially constructed forces that create it. Indeed, poststructuralist perspectives highlight the way in which any voice whose addition could potentially challenge the power relationships in the dominant discourse is likely to be acted on by that discourse (social practice, language and structures) in ways that silence the challenge. In other words, a poststructuralist perspective conceptualizes the process of adding knowledge as anything *but* straightforward. Rather, this perspective requires that the research process address and explicitly explore two dynamics that are likely to be hidden in any data set. First, it must address the impossibility of subjects "knowing" their own experience by including some form of critical analysis to reveal the limits of representation. Second, it must address the way in which experience that challenges the primacy of dominant discourse sensemaking is bound to be distorted in the process of representing it as knowledge.

Bridging these two research traditions required collecting data that would allow two different types of research analysis—a traditional qualitative method of analysis to capture experience thought to exist in some unique way in a collective (i.e., "women's voice") and a postmodern analysis to explore the systemic distortion of that experience. Because of these unique requirements the process described below is a blend of interpretive and postmodern social science research methods.

Research Process

Meeting the goals of the study as described above required three types of data. The first was a "subversive story" gathered from a nondominant group. In this case the nondominant group were female engineers who, by the nature of being both "woman" and "engineer," occupied two different and inherently contradictory subject positions in the discourse on work. As Dorothy Smith notes, it is at this line of fault between two subject positions that a critical standpoint is most likely to emerge and new knowledge can be added:

We make a new language that gives us speech, ways of knowing, ways of working politically. . . . [It provides] an opening in a discursive fabric through which a range of experience hitherto denied, repressed, subordinated, and absent to and lacking language can break out.[4]

Collecting the subversive story of these nondominant, line-of-fault subjects was done through a method of structured observation modeled on the one used by Henry Mintzberg in his 1973 study of male managers and refined by Roy Jacques in his 1992 study of female nurses.

Structured Observation

Structured observation is a data-gathering process characterized by the systematic unselective recording of events in their natural surroundings. Henry Mintzberg's structured observation of five managers in order to answer the research question "What do managers do?" resulted in the so-called "Mintzberg journals." This set of journals is perhaps the most well known example of this methodology. The advantage of structured observation over the more common self-report diary technique is that it does not require any predetermination of categories. Another, more important advantage for the purposes of this study is that it generates data about how people actually work as distinct from how they talk about the way they work. It includes behavior that subjects might unwittingly or unconsciously screen out of accounts of their workday as unimportant, trivial, or irrelevant.

Structured observation entails a straightforward, un-interpreted recording of activities that can be subjected to different forms of analysis. For example, Roy Jacques, in his detailed study of nurses as knowledge workers, used data collected in this fashion as part of a genealogical analysis, using structured observation of the time, duration, frequency, and sequence of a nurse's contact with the environment to map what he called the "enacted text" of nursing experience.[5]

This method, which carefully distinguishes between structural and interpretive data, is particularly appropriate for capturing a subversive definition of work because it provides an opportunity to observe and record concrete, situated actions that, because they stand outside the current definition of work in organizational discourse, might otherwise be invisible to both the researcher and the subject. The researcher records behavior at a micro level of detail, focusing on actions and interactions that make up different—even seemingly unrelated—elements of that behavior. The goal is to record these data in a descriptively detailed but relatively raw state so that they can be subjected to different interpretive schema.

The actual use of the method, as adapted for this study, entailed the intensive shadowing of six female design engineers. The selection of these particular six engineers was determined by organizational constraints. At the time of the study, there were only seven female design engineers in the entire product development team available for interviewing. Six were shadowed and interviewed as planned. The shadowing of the seventh, who was in manufacturing design, was aborted after two hours because my presence on the shop floor was so intrusive that note taking was impossible.

The Nature of the Shadowing

In contacting each engineer to arrange the shadowing I explained that I wanted to explore how work gets done in this environment and that I was particularly interested in the experience of people who did not fit the stereotype of a white male engineer. Probably because each was aware that others had been shadowed by different members of the research team for other aspects of the project, my request seemed to need little explanation. In fact, they seemed eager to participate, and each was extremely flexible around scheduling.

I was concerned about how my presence would affect the events of the engineer's day. Although the presence of the researcher is an issue in all participant observation, it was exacerbated in this case because the data-collection technique of unselective recording of events required extensive notetaking. I realized that having someone stand behind her, constantly writing things down, could have a marked influence on how an engineer interacted with people. Although there was no way to control for this effect, it was minimized in this case because I was already known as a researcher and had been afforded the limited "insider" status described earlier. Through my involvement with other aspects of the project, I had already met many of the people with whom the engineer interacted and as noted earlier, participants had been trained in how to act around someone who was being shadowed. As a result, introductions were rarely necessary. Rather, I experienced being acknowledged warmly, with some joking as to who was the "lucky" person being shadowed. Even when there were people whom I had not met, their nonverbal cues indicated that most knew I was a member of a research team, one of the "Ladies from the Ford Foundation," as we came to be known.

I arrived for the shadowing at 7:30 each morning and went directly to the engineer's cubicle to wait for her. Most arrived sometime around 8:00 and were thrust immediately into activity or interaction of some sort. During the day I tried to be as unobtrusive as possible, staying in the background and not getting involved in conversations directly, even with the shadowee. In an effort to make myself invisible in the interactions I witnessed, I did not make eye contact with anyone or invite them in any nonverbal way to include me in the conversation. Rather, I continued to take notes, looking up only to observe nonverbal interactions among the participants. Sometimes when the engineer and I were alone, walking to a meeting or down to the lab, I would ask a clarifying question about something that had just occurred, but for the most part, I stayed in the background, even walking a few steps behind the engineer when she walked down the halls or stopped to talk with someone. After a few hours of this I found that even when we were alone, most of the engineers would stay in the role of shadowee and would avoid engaging me in conversation.

I accompanied the subjects everywhere, even when they would tell me, for example, that they were just going for paper and would be right back. After a while they seemed to get used to this and would stop warning me about the uninteresting things they were going to do next. All of the subjects seemed to be quite conscientious about being a good shadowee, sometimes even asking me if they should do what they would normally do or do something more interesting or interactive. Nonetheless, the effect of my presence was significant in that each of them commented sometime during the day that they usually had more contact with people than they were having that day. At the end of the day, when asked whether the day's events were typical, most commented that people had not "bugged" them as much as usual.

I recorded each interaction I observed in a log, detailing the time, location, participants, and dialogue accompanying the event. The result was a log of events that represented a relatively systematic and unselective recording of each engineer's interactions with the environment—that is, all encounters with people, objects, data, and systems. At the end of the day, I used a tape recorder to capture my reactions, responses, and questions about the day's events. These transcribed tapes proved to be an unexpectedly rich source of data about the ways in which the system influenced my own understanding and interpretation of events.

Follow-up Interview

The following day an intensive interview with the shadowee was held in which I talked her through the previous days events, minute by minute. This generated a second type of data, commonly called contextualizing data. These data were expected to yield the intentions, beliefs, assumptions, and values that underlie behavior. In other words, they were intended to reveal the shadowee's sensemaking about the events that I had observed. To gather these data, I asked an open-ended question for each interaction, such as "What was this about?" or "What was going on here?" After the engineers got over their initial surprise at the level of detail in my notes, they grew quite comfortable with this contextualizing procedure. I could simply mention an incident with an uplift indicating a question (e.g., "Then Dave came by?"), and they would fill in the details.

These data were transcribed, encoded, and sorted into categories using the Ethnograph, an ethnographic software program.[6] Before I began the process, I developed a large list of potential categories based on the attributes of relational theory. This initial list changed as unused categories were discarded and new ones emerged from the data. The number and names of categories were refined using an iterative process of qualitative analysis similar to the one described by Glaser and Strauss as a "constant comparative" method of analysis.[7] It entailed continually revisiting the underlying principle of each category as new incidents were added, in order to refine the principles and allow theoretical precepts to take shape.[8]

Roundtable Discussion

When the categories had been defined so there was little overlap between them, a roundtable discussion with participants was held in which these still preliminary categories (now numbering six) were shared and reactions invited. The format for the roundtable discussion was unstructured. I simply listed the categories with examples of each and, after all six were described, asked for reactions. I used data from the roundtable discussion, which had been recorded and transcribed, to further integrate the categories, resulting in the four described in chapter 4. The process of naming the categories and the specific behaviors within each was instructive and analytic in its own right and deserves some comment.

Language and Naming

The problem I encountered in the analytic process of naming the categories and themes of relational practice helped me to further understand the dynamic process inherent in the poststructuralist concept of the "limits of language." For example, I worried that many of the activities I wanted to describe would be trivialized or sentimentalized by too close an association with the private sphere. But, of course, since the research goal was to identify behavior motivated by a relational belief system, any language to describe it had to capture this relational dimension—a dimension that is, by definition, associated with the private sphere. Although the poststructuralist framing of this study stressed this issue of language and representation as central to the research question of how relational behavior would be invisible in the dominant discourse, it was only as I struggled with naming that I began to experience the powerful dynamic inherent in the limits of representation. Trying to describe concepts such as helping, vulnerability, or empathy, when the only language available undermines or inadequately captures the essence of that concept, is a daunting task. Yet, as even the earliest theorists in the field recognized, naming is not incidental to the analysis or to the process of giving voice to marginalized experience. In one way, it *is* the task.

In poststructuralist terms, naming, or "re-presenting" experience, is an act of resistance, a concrete act of creating discursive space in which new ways of thinking about things might surface. In theoretical terms this highlights why it is so difficult to do—by definition, the dominant discourse will act to suppress any challenge to the status quo. Thus, the process of naming an experience or concept that is itself in formation can be nothing other than inadequate and incomplete. As Judith Jordan, Alexandra Kaplan, Jean Baker Miller, Irene Stiver, and Janet Surrey note in the introduction to their overview of the development of relational theory:

Many of our most difficult challenges have centered around the use of language and the attempt to find the words that best capture what we want to communicate. As we look back over these chapters, we find language used in ways with which we are no longer comfortable, but as part of the representation of the evolution of the ideas, this old and awkward language must at times remain.[9]

So, too, the names I chose for the categories of relational practice, such as the term "relational practice" itself (a term that started as "caring activity," then evolved to "relational activity," and eventually became "relational practice") are fluid and in-process. Some were borrowed from relational psychology; others were created by combining relational concepts with those of other disciplines to call attention to some aspect of the behavior I thought was distinctive or worthy of note. Readers often take issue with the names I have chosen. Some find them awkward, others find them inadequate or inaccurate. I welcome these observations because they inevitably lead to rich discussions that refine the concepts themselves.

Poststructuralist Data

For the poststructuralist analysis, a third type of data was required: a representation of the definition of work in this particular organizational setting. In framing the study I used feminist poststructuralist principles to argue that conventional definitions of real work in any organization would reflect a masculine logic of effectiveness. Within this general framework, however, I recognized that there would be differences among organizations in the degree to which this would be obvious. Schools, hospitals, and social service agencies, for example, might differ from law firms, financial institutions, or high-technology firms. For the purposes of this study, I needed a site where the masculine instrumental narrative of abstraction, rationality, and linear thinking was strong and where the implicit image of an "ideal worker" was unambiguously male. As a high-technology engineering firm, the setting met these general criteria well.[10]

Data used to represent the manifestation of the definition of work in this particular setting were gathered by the author and three other members of the research team, using the cultural diagnosis process described briefly above. Data-gathering techniques for this cultural diagnosis paralleled those suggested by Harry Levinson et al. for collecting interpretative data for organizational diagnosis, and were informed by Ed Schein's description of the elements of organizational culture.[11] For example, interview questions focused on eliciting organizational narratives that would help us understand the sensemaking frameworks people used to understand things such as the formal and informal reward systems, the attributes of "ideal" workers, the conventional definition of success, and the perception of the most pressing business problems facing the company. Along with the observational data noted earlier, these interview data were analyzed to reveal the assumptions and beliefs driving the way work was done in this environment. When the findings from the diagnosis were fed back to the organization, there was widespread agreement that they were representative of the current work culture in that group. Additional data representing the conventional definition of work as understood by the subjects themselves was obtained by analyzing the interview and round-table transcripts to reveal the inconsistencies, contradictions, and unexamined dichotomies between the traditional definition of work they embodied as members of the system and the subversive stories their observed behavior "told."

The findings from these three sources of data are reported in two parts. Part one, described in chapter 4, details the behavior, belief system, and intended effects of relational practice. Part two, described in chapter 5, identifies the way in which relational practice was brought into the dominant discourse, subjected to the truth rules of that discourse, and, ultimately, "got disappeared" as work and got constructed as something other than work.

4

Relational Practice

If there is a way of working that can be called relational practice what does it look like? What beliefs and assumptions about effectiveness does it reflect? This chapter begins to answer these questions by giving specific examples of activities that define relational practice, the underlying belief system that motivates it, and the skills it requires.

There are two things to keep in mind when reading this chapter. First, it describes only those behaviors that met relational criteria. In a search for evidence that relational practice existed, I looked for a particular kind of work behavior and a way of thinking about that behavior that indicated it was rooted in relational principles.[1] I gathered these nuggets of evidence, grouped them according to their intended effect and describe them here as relational practice. The description includes only these examples, not all the engineers' work behavior. It is not meant to suggest that the engineers practiced this way of working consistently or even primarily. Nor is it meant to suggest that these are the only types of work behaviors that might meet relational criteria. These are the work behaviors observed in this particular setting that met relational criteria.

The second thing to keep in mind is that the behavior is described from a relational perspective, as if it were one seamless story and no contradictory behaviors or competing interpretations existed. The description gathers evidence that relational practice exists—idiosyncratic, seemingly unrelated fragments of behavior that might otherwise go unnoticed—and weaves these fragments together into a story. Writing the description this way is a tactical, methodological strategy. Gathering these disparate behaviors, describing them in terms consistent with their own value system and logic, and reflecting on them as a whole, increases the ability of these behaviors to tell a "subversive story" about work, skill, and competence. In the service of this goal, the larger context of competing and contradictory interpretations is, for the moment, ignored. That is not to say the larger context is not important: On the contrary, it is central to the study and is addressed in detail in chapter 5. Nonetheless, in this chapter it is absent, requiring readers to engage in a bit of "poststructuralist paradox"—the practice of reading text *as if* it stands on its own, in order to understand how it does *not* stand on its own but is, instead, acted on by the dominant discourse. In other words, it requires that readers suspend disbelief in order to read the story from the perspective of those who are telling it, a perspective that gives the story its greatest potential to challenge mainstream thinking.

The process of telling the story began by gathering all possible examples of relationally motivated behavior and then categorizing them into four themes. The first had to do with task accomplishment, the second with enabling others, the third with self-achievement and the last with teamwork. This chapter describes selected examples of behavior in each of these categories, using quotes from the engineers[2] to describe their actions, motivations, and intended effects. The four types of relational practice are listed below:

• *Preserving:* Preserving the project through task accomplishment;
• *Mutual Empowering:* Empowering others to enhance project effectiveness;
• *Self-Achieving:* Empowering self to achieve project goals; and
• *Creating Team:* Creating and sustaining group life in the service of project goals.

The decision rule I used to assign behavior to each category was the stated or perceived primary intent of the actor, not the effect of the action. Although this was done for clarity, it tends to obscure the overlap and synergistic effects among the categories. In practice, the actions were less clearly differentiated from each other, and there were times, for example, when an activity in one category had an unintentional or secondarily intentional effect in another. I noted these overlaps when they were obvious or when I felt they added insight into the category being discussed. However, for the most part, the four categories are described as discrete, based on what the engineers themselves stated as the intended effect of the action.

Preserving

The first category, preserving, includes activities intended to preserve the life and well-being of the project by taking on tasks that would protect it from harm or prevent future problems. One way of doing this was to shoulder responsibility for tasks that were outside the technical definition of the job and doing them with the attitude of "doing whatever it takes," even if that meant putting aside a personal agenda or sacrificing some symbols of status. In the roundtable discussion one participant noticed this "hidden" aspect of a job another member was describing:

I want to make a point because you're expressing an attitude that I think is good, but it's not being called out. You have your job, and you have all these different things that have to do with your job, but you're willing to learn not just the horizontal part of your job but some of the vertical aspects of your job, too. Writing a data file isn't something that you say, "Well, that's not my job. I need a Key Op to do that, or I need a data entry person." That's one of the things that makes me mad—the whole thing of [saying], "That's beneath me, I'm not going to do that." The point is to get the function done. So I think people should be given some sort of recognition or at least let it be known that this is a positive thing. [You say to yourself] "OK, I need a new resistor on this board. The technicians are busy; I've got ten minutes." What's wrong with me picking up a soldering iron and sticking it on? Nothing. My hands aren't going to fall off.

What she calls attention to is the way a mindset of doing what needs to be done means being willing to minimize power and status differences in order to help the project. Others noted that it also means being willing to be inconvenienced by, for example, putting up with whatever procedures are necessary to get the job done, even if they are serving the needs of a "bunch of old people" rather than the needs of the task:

I will do whatever it takes to get the job done—like, at the review meetings. There are a lot of people who just won't jump through all those hoops. But I'll do whatever you say to get the change made. I want *results;* I'm not going to sit here and argue about the process. I see it [the review committee] as a bunch of old people sitting around, having to have things their way. Well, OK. They think the committee is important and all these procedures are important. All I know is, I'll do whatever it takes to get it done.

Another described extending her job laterally, picking up the slack with the attitude of "if I don't do this, no one will":

So, we were looking at it, and somebody touched one of the pictures and it screwed up; it was skewed a little bit, so they were not good enough to put in a book. And this was Friday—they were coming to pick them up. I looked at them and said, "You can't take these—there's no way. When are you going to laminate these?" He said, "I have to bring them over today." I said, "Listen, I can give you some that are good. Why don't we work on them? We'll come in tomorrow, we'll finish it, and we'll give them back. We'll bring them over Saturday, because you can't do all of them Friday night." He said, "OK, that's fine." So then Dirk [from marketing] came over and brought us pizza for lunch because we were there all day and part of the afternoon doing prints—extra prints— just so it looked good, just so that someone wouldn't come back and say, "Why did you give these out?" There was trouble, too, because I had Tony [copy-quality person] look at them, and Tony said, "I don't care." I had Tony and Carl look at them, and they shrugged, like, "Whatever." They didn't care. I'm like, I cannot *believe* they are going to let these go out the door.

So you came in on your own time?

On our own time for eight hours, Sara and I did.

And you didn't get paid for that?

We did not get paid for it. We just came in because it had to be done. If they were going to be laminated for the books, it had to be done.

The willingness to do whatever it takes to get the job done was expressed by another engineer who saw a gap in the process and filled it on her own:

Sometimes I just take responsibility for something if I can't find the right person. Like I couldn't find anyone in Manufacturing to take responsibility, so I just designed my own spares strategy. I called California and got what parts we'd need, then I sat with Manufacturing. Then I called the spares people and said, "Order these," and he did. I didn't do it to help out—I did it because it makes my job easier. But then, when it was all in place, I said to Manufacturing, "OK, now you take it over." I don't have the authority to order people to do things, so I just do them myself.

Preserving the project also meant looking at it as a whole, scanning the environment for inefficiencies, and taking the initiative to address them. For example, one engineer, in finding out that an additional software engineer had been assigned to a peripheral product, mentioned it to her boss. He shrugged as if it weren't his concern. Later in the day she followed up on it herself by calling the people involved. The next day, when I asked her about these interactions, she explained to me that she was concerned about a duplication of effort.

The point that Lois joined the team is one thing. That's good to know because we might have to talk to her about software or something. But the point that I was even more concerned about is that I heard Al talking about this test software that he's developing. But the memo said Lois was developing the software. So I wondered. It's OK as long as two people aren't working on the same thing.

Another example of looking at the whole comes from an engineer who noted that sometimes her own behavior, something as simple as a chance comment, can cause problems that go beyond her team. After hearing from a coworker that a calibration was correct, she explained why she went out of her way to drop by the lab to pass on the information:

One thing I noticed was that if you tell somebody you think there is a problem and you find out you were wrong, you better get back to them and tell them it was done right. Because they'll remember it's wrong and they'll be talking to somebody else and they'll say, "Oh, I think there might be a problem with that instrument." And it causes problems . . . so I was trying to take care of that.

Another aspect of preserving had to do with keeping the project connected to the people and resources it needed. As the following quote suggests, the willingness to do this appears to be rooted in a belief that relationships are important to the project, and keeping these relationships in good working order requires some effort. This engineer describes how she took the initiative to make sure that people who supplied valuable resources to the project, but who were not direct reports to their team, felt appreciated.

It's just that I was more sensitive to it than Ned [the manager]. Like, if someone didn't feel that it was their job, and I might have sensed they were getting to the point they were going to get hurt or feeling like they were being taken advantage of? And didn't like what they were doing? Then I've put myself in that role and I've just said to Ned, "Maybe we should send so-and-so a thank you," or whatever.

Other connecting activity involved taking an active role in maintaining existing relationships between members of the team. This form of connecting was characterized by "translating" one party to the other, either absorbing the stress or acting as a buffer between people.

Yeah, actually, people have mentioned that they have problems with Peter, the way that he gives information and [they have problems with] understanding what's going on with the belt . . . like David brought in a lot of baggage about Peter. He's always trying to find out what's going on, and he says Peter never answers the questions, and he never knows what's going on. So he's brought up the perception that you have to watch him—that Peter's not really competent, that he doesn't know what he's doing. So I'm trying to get [Peter to give] as much information as I can based on the stuff that Peter told me. So that's what you were picking up on. . . . I was just asking him questions to try to pin him down and get a better handle because sometimes I think when Peter talks he gets off on technical tangents and will just talk about how he solved a particular problem in writing this code or how they solved that electrical power problem, rather than purely giving the information that people want to hear.

In this case, "translating" Peter to others meant guiding him as he gave information so that others did not dismiss him. In addition to making sure the correct information got passed on, it also seems to have been intended to strengthen Peter's relationship with other members at the meeting, perhaps relieving them of some of the "baggage" they carried about him that caused them to dismiss him as incompetent.

For another engineer, preventing problems meant taking it upon herself to maintain ties between people who had severed their working relationship but who needed to share information for the sake of the project. When I asked her why she had called attention to some information and made sure it was included it in the minutes of a meeting, she explained that because this meeting has a reputation for being poorly run, marketing people have refused to attend:

Most of the people who used to attend and get a lot out of the meeting aren't attending because it just isn't meeting their needs. Some of the people who are not coming, when they get wind of the decisions that were made, they will try to overturn the decisions and get them changed, and that's been very frustrating. So it's getting very chaotic. So, I just wanted to caution marketing, [so they will know] there will be *no* support available after the 18th. So that's why I said to Bob, "This is worth putting in the notes."

By taking it upon herself to make sure critical information would be passed on, she tried to prevent the chaos and confusion she anticipated might result from marketing having severed its ties with operations to protest poorly run meetings.

Another way of preserving the project entailed rescuing or calling attention to problems that needed to be solved. For example, one engineer, in describing the purpose of a meeting she had attended, explained that she had identified a problem she thought was serious. She had convinced her boss and her boss' boss that it was a problem and arranged for a meeting with another division. She explained,

If I am just one person going over there to them saying, "Look, we've got this terrible problem," . . . but if we've got someone at a higher level, like Mike, who can communicate to them that it's a problem. . . . I mean, if it was just me saying it. . . . I mean, otherwise, they might not think it really is a problem. . . . But I could tell. I thought it was a really good meeting because you don't see them that wound up about problems that often, you know? They would rather dust them under the rug and say, "Look, if it's just one occurrence. . . ."

At the meeting she had taken a back seat, deferring to her boss and letting him explain her data. Her description of the meeting indicated that taking a back seat was a conscious decision to give the problem visibility and ensure that resources would be marshaled to deal with it.

What differentiates preserving behavior from other categories of relational practice is the focus on task and the relational representation of this focus as one of protection, nurturing and connecting. In this way, preserving activities are similar to what Sara Ruddick calls "preservative love,"[3] one of the three practices underlying maternal thinking. Although it might seem strange to think of the relationship between engineer and a project as similar to the relationship between mother and child, there are a number of similarities that make it an interesting analogy. In terms of dependency, the project, like the child, cannot take care of itself. By the same token, the worker, like the mother, depends on the survival of the project in order to continue to define herself as a worker.

Using the mother/child model to understand dependency highlights the way in which workers who accept responsibility for the survival of the project implicitly accept responsibility for the whole, as opposed to one small part of its well-being. A mother who is concerned about a child's physical well-being (feeding her nutritious food) but is not concerned with her intellectual growth (does not send her to school), emotional health (does not hold her or touch her), or physical safety (does not pull her from the path of an oncoming car) is unlikely to have a child who thrives or survives. This does not mean providing all the specific things a child needs—mothers cannot be at once doctor, physics teacher, psychiatrist, etc. Rather, it means making sure the connections are in place to ensure that these things will be available. Ruddick notes that mothers often hold together relationships that are important to a child's welfare, either because of the potential benefit such relationships hold— such as ties to grandparents, aunts, and teachers—or because of potential dangers such relationships hold—such as interactions with an abusive father or with institutional representatives outside the family circle (e.g., school principals, truant officers, registry of motor vehicle personnel, etc.). Thus, a mother's job is to oversee the whole, to be aware not just of those things within her control and directly related to specific actions defined as her responsibility but also to be aware of the systemic factors influencing the child's well-being and to do whatever needs to be done to influence those factors.

Likening the mother/child relationship to the worker/project suggests several interesting aspects of the belief system underlying organizational preserving activity. One, it suggests a belief in and an acceptance of responsibility for the whole. Anything that threatens the health of the project is worthy of attention. However, unlike the exclusivity of the mother/ child relationship, the project had many "parents," and it is clear these engineers expected others to assume this same sense of responsibility. The strength of this belief is evidenced by the disdain they express for those who feel their "hands would fall off" if they picked up a soldering iron or who would just shrug and let a substandard product go out the door. This expectation of integration and interdependence is another aspect of the belief system underlying organizational preserving activity. Doing one's job effectively means not only attending to specific job duties but also connecting across functions, even doing things that are beneath you in the hierarchy of job duties. This implies, of course, that good workers will have the skills needed to see things holistically and be able to operate in a context of implications and consequences rather than an atmosphere of separation and specialization.

Another assumption underlying this belief that everyone should put the project's needs ahead of individual issues such as status, hierarchy, or self-promotion, is the belief that such action will be seen as a sign of competence and commitment. Doing this without calling attention to it is part of what gave the practice its value. The engineer who sacrificed an opportunity for self-promotion and deferred to her boss in order to give a problem visibility described her action with pride, as evidence of her competence: Because of her action, they were now "wound up" about the problem. This belief that workers will gain recognition for putting the project first and being quietly competent is characteristic of relational practice.

The final dimension of the belief system underlying this practice was evidenced by the engineers' willingness to put effort into maintaining relationships they deemed critical to the project's health and vitality. Whether it meant sending thank-you notes to show appreciation, sending a peacemaker to smooth ruffled feathers, or protecting the project from the consequences of severed relationships, these activities implied a belief that the well-being of the overall project required relationships that were in good working order.

Preserving required a certain set of skills, including the ability to think contextually, anticipate consequences, and sense the emotional context of situations in order to recognize and take action when, for example, someone "might be feeling like they're getting taken advantage of."

Mutual Empowering

The second type of relational practice, mutual empowering, refers to behavior intended to enable others' achievement and contribution to the project. Although the word empower is used to describe this category, its meaning here is somewhat different from the common use of this term. In the management literature the definition of an empowered worker is one who has the information and authority to make decisions, to structure and prioritize tasks, or to improve process.[4] The relational practice described here, however, has little to do with authority and decision making. Instead, it refers to the act of enabling, or contributing to, the development of another. I chose the term empower, rather than more typical descriptors of this kind of behavior such as nurturing or helping, to highlight the fact that the behavior in this category is intended to enhance others' power and abilities. The modifier "mutual" is added to capture the notion that the practice of contributing to the development of another has a dimension of mutuality to it. Although the focus of the activity is on others, there is an implicit belief that empowering another is a mutually beneficial process. In this definition, part of what it means to contribute to another's growth is to allow that person to contribute to your own growth, whether that be emotional, relational, or intellectual.

One practice associated with this type of empowering was empathic teaching. Unlike traditional notions of teaching where the expert's knowledge dominates the interaction, empathic teaching refers to a process in which the perceived needs of the learner are paramount. It is a way of teaching that takes the learner's intellectual or emotional reality into account and focuses on the other (what does s/he need to hear?) rather than on self (what would I like to say?).

For some teaching interactions, engineers who practiced empathic teaching selected the emotional context as being the most salient feature of the interaction. They modified the way they imparted information accordingly by, for example, using collaborative language to equalize the teacher/student relationship. So information was often bracketed with phrases such as, "One of the things that might help," or "What I like to do is . . . ," or, "There may be lots of ways to do this, but. . . ." Often this collaborative language was marked by a self-deprecating tone that was consciously used to minimize the status differences inherent in teacher-student interaction. This was especially noticeable as a strategy when the teacher was in fact "one-up" in terms of hierarchy and might be expected to assume and be granted the expert role. For example, one engineer, in interacting with a young male technician who is several years her junior and two grade levels below her in the hierarchy, prefaced one of her suggestions with, "Well, this is a stupid, silly way to do this, but what I do is. . . ."

When I asked her to talk about how she teaches, she indicated that making the material less threatening or intimidating was a conscious strategy she used to increase her effectiveness:

Statistics is an expertise that people are interested in and they want to know it, but they are getting negative feedback from their managers when it takes them a long time to do an analysis or to design an experiment. So they have a lot of discouragement to learning. So if you turn them off at all, you've lost them. So in that case I always teach things so I try not to bruise an ego.

Another engineer who was teaching two male technicians in the lab sat down next to one of them and prefaced her instructions with remarks such as, "Let me show you one thing," "I don't know if I mentioned this before but," and "I know there are lots of ways to do this, but. . . ." The next day she explained it this way:

Well, the way I work with Frank is a little different. You have to be careful not to intimidate men [laughs]. I wanted Frank to feel comfortable, so that's why I sat down next to him and worked through stuff with him. It's just a style thing.

It appears that in her mind, being effective as a teacher meant responding to Frank's emotional reality both verbally (using collaborative language) and nonverbally (sitting down next to him rather than standing behind him) in order to minimize status differences that might intimidate him.

At other times the intellectual context of the situation was deemed most salient and information was modified to address this concern. For example, one engineer spent extra time creating a presentation format to make the information accessible to her audience. She notes that she considers this type of activity important to her teaching effectiveness:

I think most of [the preparation of materials] was real work. I might have a more flexible position on real work, not being a true engineer . . . I mean . . . having worked in quality which is more of a management function, trying to get people to do something. And you start seeing more of what has to get done. You see why you have to present things well. So I spent probably four hours making a graph and that was part of the analysis. But having to make the graph look nice was more a part of presenting the data. But I consider that part of getting the work done. If you are going to present some data you have to be able to present it in a way people will understand and find pleasing.

Another engineer demonstrated her consideration of the intellectual context of situations by trying to present information in ways that people would find relevant to everyday activities and tasks:

Yeah, I would do that with anybody. Some of it was just at a different level. But I've had similar discussions at a lower level where you're discussing over and over simple things like, why is there variation in my data? And I'm trying to tie in what they've heard in some class because everybody has had some class in statistics, and I'm trying to tie in "What did they learn there?" to "What am I doing now?" I'm trying to tie it back to anything they've experienced. I had a discussion recently where somebody was trying to decide—they had a class and they taught the classic exercise about "pull balls out of an urn." And they were trying to tie this to statistics, and they were like, "When would I ever use that? I hate statistics." And I said, "Well, it's like sampling machines off a line," and then I explained that it took me years to figure out where you would use "balls in an urn"! I finally figured out that it was like machines off a line. But that was the only thing I could come up with for sampling.

But there's lots of discussion like that. I'll discuss things, like, people will come and they will—one guy came, and he had data, and I said, "Well, you could do this kind of graph or that kind of graph," [pauses] but then I backed off and said, "What do you really want to know?"—because you may not need a very sophisticated statistical analysis if it's obvious in the data. But I think I always get that in-depth.

Talking through the process, explaining the thinking behind the steps as they were carried out was another way of modifying information to ensure that it would be understood and "owned" by the learner. One engineer described this type of activity as a conscious strategy:

Like, when Mark and Ed were working? They don't talk to each other—they just *do* it. Like, if they are showing you something, they don't talk while they are doing it, and if you don't know what is going on, then you are *lost*. But, like, when I was showing Cheryl, I talked the whole time so she would know what I was doing. I mean the whole thing is so that they'll be able to do it without you, right?

Although the skill of contextualizing information implies a one-directional model of teaching there was an important element of mutuality that was implicit in the way the engineers described the activity. As one noted:

Yeah, actually it sets my knowledge to . . . because I have to explain it. And I like teaching, and I like showing people something new and a new way to look at things and try to put it in their terms and such. And I get a lot out of it because I really cement my knowledge if I can explain, like, a variance. If I can explain the variance calculation to somebody in a way that they can understand it, then I understand it much better. And I've learned a lot more doing that than I learned at school taking tests and following the applied methodology.

Another way of enabling others was to keep them connected to people who were important to their achievement or success. It entailed using relational skills to smooth potentially explosive situations or rifts in other's relationships that could damage the ability of one or both of them to achieve results or be effective. Unlike the kind of connecting related to preserving the project, this protective connecting was done to enable the achievement of other people. Although these actions might ultimately have had a positive effect on the project, the primary intent was to empower.

In practice, protective connection often meant stepping in and handling a tense or difficult situation. In many cases it served the purpose of protecting people from their own lack of relational effort or ability. The behavior was illustrated vividly on one of my first days of shadowing. As we walked from the lab, the engineer's boss passed us and asked over his shoulder if she had gotten in touch with Judy yet. The next day, when I asked her about this interaction, she explained that she had taken on the job of dealing with a women on the West Coast who was difficult and who had been causing him problems.

Oh, Mike was just reminding me to call her. She's this person who has a bad personality. She just always blames other people for whatever is going wrong. If you call with a question, she doesn't just give you an answer, she immediately starts saying why "so and so" is responsible for it. Mike was getting really frustrated with her, so I said, "Let me deal with her," and I took over getting the information from her. I said, "I'll beat her at her own game." So I told her that I'm the person who cleans things up, who organizes them.

It was evident in her voice that she took pride and pleasure in using her relational skills in this way. I asked her if this was a formal part of her job—was it now part of her goals and objectives? She dismissed this suggestion and said that, no, it was just a way to help out.

Another form of protective connecting entailed protecting people from the consequences of their own lack of relational skill or effort. For example, Abby and her partner Sam were working in the lab when their boss came in. The boss asked a question of Sam, who did not look up from what he was doing and did not answer. Abby looked from one to the other. Then Sam said, "That's not our job anymore; why don't you ask Katie?" But before he could even finish the comment, Abby jumped in and gave the boss the information he requested. He said thank you and left. Abby didn't comment on the interaction. Sam continued to work but started to whistle nonchalantly. The next day, when I asked her about this incident, she explained:

That was part of the problem I was explaining before, that we wanted that project and we lost it? [Our boss] lost it to that other group. So that was [Sam using] a little sarcasm there saying, "Hey, you guys—you didn't fight enough for it, so now you go talk to Katie about it. She's in charge of it." So that was the little zinger. But I could tell by Carl's voice that he was upset, and Sam sometimes, like, [makes a grinding noise] twists the knife in harder and harder. So I just jumped in and answered the question. Sam does that. . . . If he really doesn't want to help you, he won't help you—*end of story.* So I'm the middleman who goes, "OK, this is the reason," sort of like a tension breaker, solving two problems at once, I guess.

Another type of protective connecting was being aware of a person's relationship with someone and taking care not to jeopardize or disrupt it. For example, at one point Jim came into the office and handed Ann a packet of papers and said, "Carl [the boss] gave me this. It needs to be edited by tonight or first thing tomorrow morning." He then handed her the sheaf of papers, and she began going through it. He stayed marginally involved, working on his computer while he listened to her comments as she edited. At one point, she looked up and noticed the boss coming down the hall. She hid the sheaf of papers and started working on her computer. The next day, when I asked her about this incident, she said she was trying to hide the fact that she was helping Jim because the boss might think this help was inappropriate or might think less of Jim because of it:

At first I wasn't sure because sometimes Jim will say, "You read it," and then Carl will come in and say to Jim, "I gave that to *you* to read [edit]; why is she reading [editing] it?"

Enabling others also took the form of eliminating barriers, both emotional and practical, that might hinder someone's ability to achieve or be effective. Responding in this way often meant cutting others slack because of some emotional situation they were dealing with, even if the situation were outside the work context. For example, this engineer explains why she did not get upset when someone snapped at her:

Well, he is just in a bad mood. His wife is pregnant, and it's tense. . . . He can't even go to the pizza party this afternoon because he has to take her to get an ultrasound.

Another explains why she can take it in stride when a peer tries to control a meeting she is running:

He just has a hard time, especially with women. My old manager used to tell me that there are three things that show power in this culture. The first is controlling meetings, the second is controlling floor space, and the third is the number of people reporting to you. So he is just feeling left behind, and he has to show power somehow. It doesn't bother me.

And another works hard at putting herself in a coworker's shoes. Although she expresses her frustration with his inability to do the job effectively, she recognizes that the task facing him is more difficult than the one she undertook in a similar job. At first she expresses anger but then she reflects on his situation and notes that she has some sympathy with the situation he is in:

He should know which things would have been [given a] green [light], of course. It's so fundamental I hardly knew where to start telling him. So I was real frustrated with that one [pauses]. It was sort of enlightening to me at one point, though, when he said that he's trying to pull together an assessment when he's never even sat through one. I have sympathy with that problem. At the very least, even though I didn't know how to [do the job], at least I knew what the [review] process was. I knew why it existed. So you can see the problem [he has]. I mean, I think he is just flailing around, totally in the dark.

Removing practical barriers was more straightforward and entailed responding to direct requests for help. As one engineer said, "When someone asks me for something and I'm not the person they need, I make sure I find out who that person is, or I offer to take them there." This way of extending the help beyond the original request was demonstrated by others who did things such as offer to make a call to find out the information, get up from a chair to find a pad of paper for someone rather than simply point out where it was, or offer to do the job when asked to help with part of it.

Sometimes eliminating practical barriers meant giving people the information they needed, helping with a problem, or answering a question without giving someone a hard time for asking. In talking about this kind of activity, it was clear that the engineer's willingness to help others came from a belief in interdependence, a mindset that saw needing help as part of the human condition, not as evidence of individual deficiency. As this engineer notes, needing help is part of the job:

But everyone should feel like that. Because if everyone knew everything, we all wouldn't be here, you know? We all know something that other people don't know, so it shouldn't [be a big deal]. People should realize that. But some people don't, though.

This belief in the inevitability of interdependence was further demonstrated by their frustration with those who tried to make others feel bad for asking for help. At the roundtable, three of the engineers agree that this is a common practice that has a predictable result: Only some people get asked for help.

E1:   I also think it's easier—my opinion—for a man to come to a woman and say, "Can you show me this?" than go to another man. Because I've noticed in my area, people will tend to come to me if they don't understand something. But if they need a direct answer, they will go to someone else. It's like if [they need someone] to show them how to do something, they'll come to me. I'm like, "Well, if this person just gave you the information, why are you asking me? Any other time you'd go to this other person."

E2:   Or they will ask me and I'll say, "Sure, what do you need help with?" But if they ask a guy, they'll tease them about it before they help them—like, "Oh, come on, how can you not know how to do that?" And it won't be malicious, but it will be teasing.

E1:   Enough to make you not want to go to that person again.

E3:   It's admitting that you don't know something.

E2:   Even if it doesn't bother you, if it doesn't make you feel bad and it's not intended that way. What's easier? To go to somebody who's going to say, "Sure, what do you need help with?" Or to go to someone who teases? . . . Even if it's some good-natured teasing, it's easier to go to the person where there's no teasing at all.

They recognize that although they believe reciprocity is implied in giving someone help or cutting someone slack, there are those who do not assume any reciprocal responsibility. For example, this engineer talks about how she has learned that, for many of the people there, if you help them out, they think you are naïve and don't know any better:

If you try to nurture, they just don't get it. They don't understand that is what you are doing. They see it as a weakness, and they use it against you. They don't see that you are doing it consciously. . . . They think you have missed something or that they've gotten something over on you. So if you try to be nice, you end up doing other people's work. I've gotten so that now I say, "OK, look, I'll help you out on this one. *But you owe me one.*"

This quote reveals an interesting dynamic. She realizes that her belief in reciprocity and interdependence is not universal and that she has to be direct in order to reinforce the fact that doing something indirectly or invisibly—helping without making the other's need obvious—does not mean she is unaware she is giving help. Rather, she realizes that she is giving help and believes this is normal and reasonable because everyone needs help. Since he seems to miss what she sees as this critical part of the helping message—I'll help you without making a big deal of it now, if you will help me without making a big deal of it later—she has to spell it out for him with a "you owe me one."

Eliminating barriers often meant something as simple as sharing information. Sometimes the reason for sharing information was to help people prepare or arm them with information they might need in the future. For example, this engineer generalizes from a single request and goes out of her way to distribute information people might find useful:

Over e-mail I saw a request for information on Novell. I don't know much about it, but I know my husband does. So I asked him about it, and he wrote something up, and now I will distribute it to people.

Sometimes the reason for sharing information was more protective and was done to alert someone to a potentially threatening or uncomfortable situation, such as the following example of an engineer who passes on what she knows to protect a coworker from being blindsided at a meeting with his boss:

Yeah, I was just telling him about [the belt problem]. . . . He would find out about it at the [review] meeting on Thursday when [his boss] is scheduled to go in and talk to him.

In summary, mutual empowering activities enabled others to produce, achieve, and accomplish work-related goals and objectives. It was characterized by a willingness to put effort into what Cato Wadel calls embedded outcomes.[5] These are outcomes embedded in other people, such as increased competence, increased self-confidence, or increased knowledge. What differentiated these activities from other types of relational practice was this focus on empowering another person. Unlike the previous theme of preserving, which is analogous to dependency in a mother/child relationship model, the theme of empowering draws on a model of relational interaction characterized by interdependence and fluid power relations. Mutual empowering behavior appears to be rooted in the belief that outcomes embedded in others are worth working for and that everyone needs and should be able to expect this kind of help. As one engineer said, "But everyone should feel like that."

The process of mutual empowerment reflects a concept of power and expertise that is fluid, where dependence on others is assumed to be a natural, but temporary, state. Implicit in this is an expectation that others should adopt this attitude and be willing to give and receive help because there are benefits to be gained in each role. The notion of mutuality was evident in the way the engineers spoke of enabling activities not as altruism, but as something that enhanced their own self-esteem and self-efficacy. In fact, it was part of what it meant to be good at your job. As one engineer noted:

I know I'm doing a good job when people think of me when they have a problem. I've succeeded when people think of me as someone who is (1) competent and (2) someone who will help. Most people around here only care about the first thing—competence. They don't care if they are seen as approachable. I do.

Mutual empowerment activities require an ability to operate in an environment of "fluid expertise," where power and expertise shifts from one party to the other, not only over time but in the course of one interaction. This requires two skills. One is a skill in empowering others: an ability to share—in some instances even customizing—one's own reality, skill, and knowledge in ways that make it accessible to others. The other is skill in *being* empowered: an ability and willingness to step away from the expert role in order to learn from or be influenced by the other. Expecting mutuality in this type of interaction implies an expectation that others will have both sets of skills and will be motivated to use them, regardless of the individual status of the parties involved. In this, the engineers were often disappointed, as others often "just don't get it."

This discussion suggests two important aspects of the relational belief system underlying and motivating the practice of mutual empowering. First, it can be seen as an expression of a belief in mutuality and interdependence, a belief in the naturalness of moving from the "enabler" to the "enabled" role with no loss of self-esteem because each role has the potential to enhance self-worth. Thus, engaging in empowering activities in this belief system is worthy of time and effort because it is an occasion of growth, achievement, and development for both parties involved. It contributes to valuable outcomes embedded in others (skills, knowledge, and information) and valuable outcomes for oneself (an opportunity to learn from others and an opportunity to enhance one's interacting, or relational, sense of self).[6]

Second, this conceptualization of empowering as mutual suggests that such activity is undertaken with an expectation of reciprocity, i.e., an expectation that others will be similarly motivated to empower and will have the skills to do so. An expectation of reciprocity implies a belief that others will have the ability and willingness to empower (i.e., to present knowledge in ways that make it accessible) and to be empowered (to be open to learning from you and acknowledging that they have learned).

The effort engineers were willing to expend to keep people connected to one another seems to indicate two complementary beliefs: (1) that growth *can* occur for both parties in relational interactions, and (2) that connection is so essential to growth and achievement that negative consequences will occur if the connection is severed.

Another aspect of the belief system underlying empowering activity is the belief that responding to individuals in ways that will enable them to achieve must include both emotional and practical considerations. Enacting this belief requires an ability to empathize with another person's reality and recognize it as different from one's own.

Self-Achieving

The third category of relational practice, self-achieving, refers to using relational skills to enhance one's professional growth and effectiveness.

One type of activity in this category had to do with maintaining connections with coworkers in ways that would preserve the future growth potential of these relationships. Implicit in this behavior was the belief that relationships are important to growth and achievement and that the long-term benefits of maintaining and nurturing affiliations with others outweigh the costs. Making an effort to quickly repair potential or perceived breaks in working relationships was one way of maintaining healthy connections. This type of re-connecting was characterized by things such as following up with someone after a disagreement in a meeting or going out of the way to track someone down who might be feeling hurt or slighted. What was striking about these activities was the distress and sense of urgency to "make things right" that accompanied them.

For example, one engineer, in the context of a light, bantering conversation with a colleague about what she was learning in school, insisted that a certain protocol for coding was correct. The colleague looked surprised but conceded the point and after a few minutes, left the office to return to her desk. The engineer started having second thoughts about what she had said and took out a book to verify the information. When she found out she was mistaken she seemed quite distressed. She got up from her desk and left the office to look for her colleague but could not find her. She went back to working on her computer but every few minutes would look up and announce to no one in particular, "I have got to find Kelly and tell her she was right." This sense of urgency to make things right was different from the desire to correct misinformation about the project that was described earlier. The information exchanged in this case was generic, related to the field of engineering but not in any direct way that endangered the project. Rather, the urgency seemed to spring from the break in the relationship, the fact that she had invoked the expert role but was wrong and could not rest until things were set right.

For another engineer the urgency to re-connect sprang from a social faux pas. In the morning as we were walking through the halls, she inadvertently called another engineer by the wrong name. As soon as he was gone she realized her mistake and seemed annoyed with herself, muttering how stupid it was. A few minutes later when we got to the lab and he was there, she made a point of calling him by name. Four hours later, when we were in another lab and he came in, she jokingly recalled having called him the wrong name and recounted a story of how she once got quite angry with someone who couldn't remember her name, and now she is getting her comeuppance because she had done it herself. Talking about it directly seemed to clear the air and re-establish the relationship on firm ground. At any rate, both laughed about the incident and began working together on the machine.

Theories of growth-in-connection suggest that this urgency to reconnect stems from a belief in the long-term potential of relationships that are in good working order. In this model, the "fear" of separation stems from a desire to avoid conditions that might preclude future growth. One engineer talked about this type of avoidance behavior as a conscious strategy:

I get my point across, sometimes indirectly . . . the more it bothers me the more indirect I get. If I feel that confronting the issue may end the relationship, I won't confront it.

Lyn Brown and Carol Gilligan speak of this type of relational activity as a paradoxical move *out* of relationship for the *sake* of relationship.[7] That is, not speaking your mind, while it might appear to preserve the relationship, is an act of distancing and inauthenticity that undermines mutuality because it assumes unequal investment in the connection. For example, if one party sacrifices voice to preserve connection, it assumes that the other is not up to the task of furthering the relationship through listening, understanding, and responding. The engineer above added another dimension to Brown and Gilligan's notion of the paradox when she silenced her voice in stages, first speaking more and more indirectly to minimize the negative impact of direct confrontation, until finally, after making an assessment that the relationship is in jeopardy, she stops. In effect, she decides not to pursue growth in the current interaction but preserves the possibility of future growth by not severing ties completely. Relational theory suggests that the motivation to invest effort in maintaining connection springs from a belief that collaborative conditions are necessary, perhaps even essential to growth. For example, one engineer explains that her motivation to remain connected to others springs from her desire to create an environment in which she can achieve, develop, and grow:

At least for me personally, I'm not somebody who feels very comfortable negotiating in an atmosphere of conflict. I like to talk about things, explain why I think something, hear about what the other person thinks about something. So if I can keep it from ever getting elevated to that [confrontational level], then I can be working in an atmosphere that is more comfortable for me.

For another, effort expended in maintaining a reciprocal helping relationship is seen as a wise investment:

In my experience, if you really help somebody out, it comes back to you tenfold. Because if I have a problem, say, I help somebody out because their machine is broken and I help them figure out what the problem is. Then my machine breaks in an area that they work on. I'm much more likely to get parts that I really shouldn't have gotten or somebody's time to come and look at it when they are not being allocated for that. So I think it really does pay you back much more than the time you put in to help people.

For yet another, it is a way of ensuring that she will get the information she needs to do her job effectively:

Because some of them . . . I think they might call me first just because they like me—or whatever. After I fix [the machine] I can help them with a crossword puzzle—or whatever. Or, there are a few of them, one in particular, who looks out for me. Not looks out for me exactly, but if he sees a problem, he says, "Hey, have you seen this?" And he calls me over so I would just know about it.

Reflecting, a second type of self-achieving behavior, entailed paying attention to the emotional overlay of situations in order to understand what was happening and what the most effective response should be. Sometimes this meant accessing one's own feelings—a type of self-reflection—as a source of data. For example, one engineer used "feeling bad" to understand the dynamics of getting recognized at meetings. This helped her understand her own behavior and also helped her recognize the need to develop a strategy to get what she wanted in a way that would feel better:

I have been thinking about this a lot lately. This isn't true confessions, but I came to a realization that I was being rude in meetings . . . *a lot* . . . and I didn't like it because I didn't feel good [about it]. And I was pondering, "Why am I doing that?" Because it doesn't feel good, but I am still doing it. So there is something else rewarding me. . . . And it was the getting noticed. It was the easiest, fastest, simplest way to get noticed. And once you are noticed, you get heard. But since it doesn't feel good, I really want to find a different way that is still effective.

This type of self-reflection is a key element of experiential learning and is thought to differentiate those who learn from experience from those who do not.[8] In this case understanding the situation depended on an ability to understand and appreciate the complexity of one's own feelings and a skill in staying with the contradictory information—feeling good about getting recognized, feeling bad about how it was done—until an action that might resolve the contradiction evolves.

Another type of reflecting relied on the ability to understand others' feelings and emotional responses and modify one's own behavior in response. For example, in the following situation, the engineer used her appreciation of the power of feelings as determinants of behavior to understand why inefficiencies at meetings appeared to be encouraged by the chief engineer:

I really felt that part of the problem was the behavior of the chief engineer, that he actually encouraged a lot of the inefficiencies in the meetings because when you would try to facilitate around it as a participant in the meeting, he would not support you. He would support the people who were causing the problem. So it was a problem in my mind; it was obviously not a problem in his mind. He liked it going that way, and I thought a lot about it at the time because why would this person who I respect a lot let this go on and actually encourage it? And I finally concluded that it was because he learned a lot of information that way, for himself personally, that he would never learn in a more structured environment, and he was very much an engineer at heart and wanted to know that stuff. Whether he really needed to know it or not is a subject of discussion, but he wanted to know it, so he liked to have that behavior go on. . . . If you are really at heart still an engineer and you can't stand to let go of it, you're very happy to spend twenty minutes bending your mind around a technical problem because it feels good. . . . I think there's a lot of frustrated engineers running these programs.

Understanding the strength and power of the feeling motivating what she saw as inefficient behavior caused her to modify her own response to it:

I would try in subtler ways to make it happen, but whenever I even touched on the subject of meetings being inefficient, there was usually pretty immediate resistance to any kind of change. It was sort of, "This is how programs are managed, this is how they've always been managed, this is how we have been successful and who are you—little, tiny, new kid on the block, thirty-year-old female—who are you to tell us that we're doing something that could be improved upon?" And that was, you know, it was OK. I'll just compromise and not argue about it because it's not going to get me very far.

There were many instances where engineers modified their own behavior in response to the emotional context of a situation by cutting someone some slack. In this case, cutting slack seemed to be motivated not so much by a desire to enable the other person, as in mutual empowering behavior, but rather to enable *herself* by eliminating a barrier that could overwhelm her ability to achieve. For example, one engineer who, in explaining to me the context of a meeting I had witnessed, described how her boss would often ask her to take charge of things but then, in meetings, would override her decisions and make it clear that he was in charge. She explained that she sees his confusing behavior as coming from his emotional need to be seen as in control, especially to those who are above him in the organizational hierarchy. This understanding seemed to help her "work around it":

Yeah, Tim's just like that. He's asked me to do lots of things and then doesn't really want to let go of them. Yeah, he's just like that. So he wants me to come in with the agenda, document the whole meeting, keep it on track, but at the same time he doesn't really want to give up control, or not run it himself. . . . In terms of impacting productivity or anything like that, I'm used to it because I understand him now because I've been working with him for a little while. . . . And I think it has to do with my being junior and the fact that in the presence of other people he wants to—I don't know—make it clear. Like, I don't know if you noticed the change when Fred came in. Because Fred has, I don't know, more influence maybe. So changing his behavior when someone senior comes in, you know, that's what he does. Anyway, I think I can work around it and I try not to let it bother me.

Another engineer used the same technique when she shared information about a problem she was working on with someone who came into the lab angrily demanding to know what was going on. The next day she was able to put the incident in a larger context:

Well, I [told him about the problem] because I think he feels a little territorial about it. He thinks of the lab as his area. Also, the meeting I have with him later is to get information from him that [our boss] wants me to document because she wants it documented in my style. Technically, this is his job so I don't think he feels real comfortable with that, so he may be a little threatened, and that may have something to do with his coming in here now and wanting to know.

Her ability to reflect on the emotional overlay of what might be considered an annoying request for information allowed her to respond willingly to his need to be involved. The decision to share the information rather than withhold it appears to have been an intentional strategy to enhance her own effectiveness by increasing the chance that the meeting they have later on in the day would be productive. As she indicated later in the interview, she uses the practice of reflecting on the emotional context of situations and modifying her behavior in response to it as a conscious strategy. And she expresses her amazement that others do not use this relational skill to enhance their effectiveness:

[Engineers are] intelligent—why can't they get it? I sit in meetings and I watch people alienate the people they need to do stuff for them, and I think, "There is no way that person is going to say what you need him to say now because you just made him look like a jerk." They don't know the way to get someone to see things your way is *not* to call him stupid!

The third type of relational practice used to foster self-achievement was relational asking, a way of asking for help that increased the likelihood help would be given. It was relational in that it took the emotional landscape of the interaction into account, paying attention to one's effect on others and thinking about the needs and emotional context of all the parties involved. It is a practice rooted in assumptions about mutuality and reciprocity. Virginia Held, in using mothering to develop an alternative to contractual models of thinking, speaks of this type of practice as an exercise of power, the power to call forth tenderness in another.[9] She notes that although we often think of power in a helping interaction as being a relationship between the powerful and the powerless, the exercise of power in such interactions is actually more mutual and two-directional. Recognizing this characteristic of mutuality adds a different dimension to the concept of helping that gives rise to a certain practice— a certain way of asking—that is different from the norm. In the roundtable discussion, one engineer's description of the norm is so accurate that laughter erupts before she can make the contrast.

If there's something [pauses]—if I had to come to you to ask for help, I think a lot of guys would say, "Katie, I'm in a position of leadership over you, and you have to do this for me. Make these files." And if you don't do it, then they'll go to [your boss] and say, "Katie wouldn't make these files." [Group laughs.] And I tend to like to say, "Katie, can you show me how to do one of these?"

This relational way of asking appeared to be a natural outgrowth of a belief in the inevitability of interdependence. When needing help is seen as a universal human condition and not as an individual deficiency, then asking for help is not something to be avoided. In fact, rather than viewing "not knowing" as an embarrassment, in this context it can be seen as an invitation, an opportunity to practice the relational skill of enabling. Making visible one's "not knowing" is a way of calling forth enabling behavior in others. There were many examples of this way of asking for help, in which the request was prefaced by a declaration of "not knowing," which called forth a tender or enabling response. Statements such as, "Look, some of this is wrong, I didn't know what I was doing," or "Well, I'm batting 0 for 2 today," or "This is as far as I can go with this problem" served that purpose.

The emotional tone was not the only thing that characterized this practice and differentiated it from other ways of asking for help. Another distinguishing characteristic was the kind of help sought. Implicit in the request was a recognition that the help would be used to enable and empower the seeker, not as a way of avoiding responsibility. Thus, one engineer described how the quality specialist did not mind teaching her things because he knew she would teach others in her group. He was willing to invest time in her because he was confident she would invest time in others and serve as a resource to her group rather than hoard the information:

So now, instead of everybody going to him from my group, now I can do them for my group. I think I have people who feel like that about me, like they would really help me a lot because now instead of them having to do the work, I'm doing the work my group needs.

This is fundamentally different from asking for help in order to take advantage of another person's willingness to shoulder responsibility. For example, this engineer describes her discomfort with being asked for help—not to empower another to do a job more effectively, but to do the job for him:

One of the things that's been coming up is, with a new person in the group—there's this guy starting—he has to develop test plans for a new product. So he's relying heavily on what we know, which is fine. But what I see is that he's not only relying on it, he's expecting us to do the work. And some of the work does not require our expertise. It's setting up a report on the Star, setting up a lot of clerical, computer work to get a report out. I'm like, he could do that, but he is pushing it off. And I'm like, this is not real work for me because it's something he could do. I'm not adding any expertise to doing that part of it. That's something I'm tied up with right now, trying to divide that up and get that part pushed back on him.

Others express this same frustration with what they see as a lack of differentiation between empowering helping and exploitative helping:

Yeah, like, in the morning he'd come in, instead of giving me technical stuff or engineering stuff, he'd come in and say, "Can you take this in for me?" And I would look at him, and Ed would say, "She's not your damn secretary." At first Ed would be the one to say something because I was like, "Well, whatever. . . . What's once in a while, right?" But then it got to be constant, and I said that I'm not doing it. And he would say, "I thought we were a team. I have a meeting to go to." And I'd say, "That's not my problem. This is part of your objectives, not part of my objectives." I mean, really . . . you can't always give somebody your work. It's OK to do it once in a while . . . that is not a problem. But you can't always do that.

In summary, self-achieving activities were those in which engineers used relational skills to enhance their own effectiveness. It was this focus on the self and the use of relational skills to strategize their own efficacy, that differentiated this practice from other categories of relational practice. Implicit in these activities was the belief that not just personal, but professional growth is rooted in connection and that the long-term benefits of maintaining a relationship are worth the effort. Relational theory suggests that the urgency to prevent or mend disruption is indicative of a belief that severed relationships have potentially negative effects that should be avoided.[10]

Spending time and effort reflecting on the emotional complexity of situations indicates a belief that emotions are an important source of information, both about oneself and about situations. Using these emotional data to understand ambiguous or confusing circumstances helped the engineers develop what they perceived as more effective strategies in dealing with situations. It allowed them to choose their battles and to avoid unintentionally creating obstacles to their own effectiveness and ability to achieve results. Finally, the practice of relational asking implies a belief in a particular definition of interdependence, where asking for help is not a sign of weakness, but an invitation to empower. The ability to differentiate it from other forms of asking suggests that this practice was a conscious decision, a strategy designed to increase the likelihood they would get the empowering outcome they sought.

In terms of skills, self-achieving behavior requires emotional competence: an ability to access emotional data and the skill in understanding the implications and complexity of these data. It also requires an ability to stay with contradictory information—feeling good about getting recognized, feeling bad about how it was done—so that a new strategy might evolve. Thus, it requires an ability to engage in holistic thinking and to blend thinking, feeling, and action in a way that bridges the rational/emotional divide.

Creating Team

Creating team is a category of activities intended to foster group life. It differs from what is generally thought of as team building because it is concerned with creating a generalized *experience* of team rather than the more typical task of creating team *identity*. Traditional team building activities are assumed to be the responsibility of the team leader and include things such as setting boundaries, determining lines of authority, setting goals, or defining tasks. In contrast, working to create the experience of team is leadership of a different sort. Activities in this category are more generalized and were intended to create the background conditions in which group life could flourish. The intention was not to enhance one's personal relationships (although they might have that effect), or to enable others (although they might have that effect), or to manage group process but to create baseline relational conditions necessary for growth-in-connection.

There were two types of activities in this category—those focused on individuals within the collective and those focused on the collective itself. Attending to the individual was expressed through practices that acknowledged others' unique preferences, problems, feelings, and circumstances. This included sending verbal and nonverbal messages of affirmation such as maintaining eye contact when others were talking, nodding, smiling, or making encouraging comments such as, "right," "good point," "OK, good" or even just "yeah" and "uh huh." Pamela Fishman notes that this type of response during conversation is the maintenance work of conversational interaction and demonstrates an appreciation of and involvement with the speaker.[11] Each engineer evidenced behavior of this sort in abundance. Many times during meetings she would be the only person making eye contact with the speaker. My field notes are sprinkled with comments about such verbal and nonverbal affirming behavior. Interestingly, it seemed to occur regardless of hierarchical status. Even when the person speaking in a meeting was subordinate to the engineer, the nodding, eye contact, and nonverbal affirmation continued.

Sometimes attending to the individual meant listening and responding with empathy to non-work-related information. For example, this engineer explains why she took time to listen to a coworker's rambling story:

The other thing is, because men joke around so much with each other, when a man does have something he wants to talk about he won't go to another man . . . he'll go to a woman. I've had men who I know don't even like me use me to vent about really personal things. Like, this one guy I know doesn't like me, and I don't like him much, started to talk about the fertility problems he and his wife were having. I mean, that's heavy stuff. And I've talked to several women who say that men come in and sit down and talk to them. You don't really have to say anything, just listen. They just want someone who will listen and not joke around about it. I feel bad when others are feeling bad or having a hard time, and I know it's not going to kill me to spend some time with them. And also, who else are they going to go to? It doesn't cost me anything, really, just to listen. But sometimes it just feels like a big responsibility because even if you are not really in the mood, you *have* to do it. I mean, if they are coming to you, it must be pretty bad, and where else can they go?

She felt her response was, indeed, work. At times it "just feels like a big responsibility," and she responded empathetically, although she was fully aware that "he doesn't like me, and I don't like him much." Nonetheless, she took it upon herself to respond to him in a way that would validate and acknowledge his feelings.

She was not alone in expressing the belief that listening to feelings is an important aspect of fostering group life. This engineer responded in a similar way to a coworker who wandered into her cubicle and began talking to her as she worked at the computer. He began by asking her a question. He then mentioned something about his dad and his dad's company, which is a competitor of this company. She nodded and smiled encouragingly, not saying much, just listening. He then went on to talk about his own experience of working for this other company and how they did things right. The exchange lasted only a few minutes. The next day, when I asked her about it she said:

Sometimes I think, "You haven't worked there for thirty years, why do you still talk about it?" He was only there for a few years and then he was laid off in one of those layoffs, which we don't think of back in the '60s. So I think he—I don't know if he feels bad that he got laid off or what, but he always goes on and on about how well they did things. . . . He's a person who really likes some interaction. I think one of the things that scares him about retirement is, who is he going to talk to? So he'll come over and talk to me. I notice he goes in and talks to Dorothy sometimes, too. He just sits down and starts talking about something [laughs] . . . and he's not worried about whether you have a lot to do and so forth. That's just how he is.

Taking the time to listen to his experience because he is someone who "likes interaction" acknowledges his need to be seen as unique, someone with a past that extends beyond the present environment.

During the roundtable discussion, the engineers described this type of response as a conscious strategy to enhance team spirit. One sums up the discussion, agreeing that being aware of feelings is important to team effectiveness.

I agree with you—the more team-spirited people are more effective in what they're doing. And I equate being conscious of other people's feelings with working in a team spirit. I think people are much more effective this way.

Relational theory supports this view and suggests that individuals who feel understood and accepted are more likely to be accepting of others, leading to a kind of group life characterized by what Jean Baker Miller and Irene Stiver call a "zest" for interaction and connection.[12]

There were some instances in which engineers extended this type of empathic response from an expressive to an instrumental act, responding behaviorally to others' needs and preferences. Examples cited in the mutual empowering section above, in which engineers modified their behavior in order to cut someone slack, are instances of this behavior. Cutting slack, particularly in response to the emotional context of a situation, can be thought of as a type of instrumental affirmation and validation of others' uniqueness. As such, it has the potential not only to enable individual achievement by eliminating potential emotional barriers, it also can create esprit de corps, a sense that others are concerned about one's ability to achieve. This in turn can create the reality of interdependence, i.e., opportunities for collaboration and cooperation.

For example, this engineer explains why, although she is responsible for a part of the project that has the potential to be "high visibility," she understands and can respond to the previous coordinator's expressed desire to stay involved.

He's still interested in EPOCH. When I first came aboard, they were having this flatness problem, and Paul was glad to hand over the responsibility to me. But he was the one who started it, so he's always interested in it. He could just be the AZT guy and not handle any concerns about EPOCH. But when they gave me EPOCH, he kind of said, "Don't shut me out; I've been working on EPOCH for years and I want to be involved with it."

She understands his desire to be involved with this part of the project stems in part from a fear of moving to something new that may not have the same potential for visibility. So she invites him to participate in ways that add to the effectiveness of the project and help her out:

AZT is kind of uncharted territory—we don't really know how it's going to work and if it will work in our machine or not. So we're not 100% committed to going to it yet . . . so he just wants to stick close to EPOCH, and I'm glad to let him help because sometimes he really helps; like, when I'm really feeling buried, he'll take something, and it really helps.

Other instances of responding to preferences were more routine, such as one engineer volunteering to crawl around, under, and over machines to get serial numbers while her partner recorded the information because "he doesn't like doing it . . . it's no big deal" or another engineer volunteering to take on the data-entry phase of a project and taking it home to work on because it is "mindless work" you can do in front of the television and "no one likes to do it."

Interactions such as these, which validate and affirm individuals, either through empathic listening or actively responding to individual needs, circumstances, and preferences, can be thought of as creating conditions *within* individuals that foster group life. In contrast, attending to the collective, the second type of behavior in this category, entailed creating conditions *among* people in order to create an environment that would foster collaboration and cooperation. These activities include facilitating difficult situations by using one's interpersonal skills to absorb stress or reduce conflict and envisioning or creating structural practices that would encourage relational ways of working.

Facilitating entailed handling difficult situations or supplying the interpersonal skills that were needed to keep things on an even keel. It is recognized by some of the engineers as an activity that those with relational skills are often expected to do:

What I see around here is that women get men to talk to each other. I think women are inherent facilitators. I can't think of any women I work with who are not good at getting a team together. In fact, I've never thought of this before, but often some pretty high-level people will stop by my office and ask me, or other women, to do this kind of thing [facilitate communication]. I mean, they don't phrase it this way; they sort of drop by to talk about this problem they're having, and that just seems to be part of the solution. Although I have to say that there are so few women here that it's hard to tell if this is really a male/female thing. It may be that happens to males who are facilitators, too. But it does happen to women.

Sometimes facilitating took the form of absorbing the stress or tension generated by conflict or the threat of conflict. For example, this engineer explains how she volunteered to work second shift to avoid what she later called "battling for resources."

For a while I was working, like, to help them out in a pinch. They had this huge backlog of all these developer specs that had to be closed. And Roy was doing a lot of that work, and so was Mike. So they gave everyone who volunteered a couple of these specs to close, which is really a lot of work. And it all had to be done on the Star [computer]. Ray and I share a Star, and Don was using his, and John was using his, so there was this battle. It didn't make sense. So I worked second shift for a whole week so that Ray could use the Star during the day, and then I could use it second shift.

Are you the one who came up with the solution of working second shift?

Yeah, nobody would really require you to work second shifts, although I think once Ray had to work second shift once a week one time to support the line. But they would never, in our group, make you work second shift for a whole week. But [laughs] if you volunteer they take you up on it.

Sometimes facilitating meant absorbing stress created by the fact that they were women in a male environment. They recognized that this was difficult for men to accept and could cause problems. So they spoke of devising ways to get what they needed without being confrontational since men "don't like losing to a woman," and they spoke of it being "no big deal" to be called "that engineering broad" because as one woman put it:

I mean, these guys have their problems, too. They aren't crazy about women engineers anyway, and then to have a female engineer [out on the floor]. It's just too much.

Many, like this engineer, spoke of using humor to defuse a potentially uncomfortable situation, avoid confrontation, or help someone save face:

I've had my share of things. . . . We had one meeting where they were talking about getting rid of the old Key Ops for a test and getting new ones. And how'd they put it? They said, "Well, shall we get rid of the old Key Ops?" and one guy said, "I'd like to keep the young girls on"—he was joking—and everybody started laughing, and then they saw me and they stopped. And they froze. So it was completely in my hands how the situation was going to go. And I said, "Well, I kind of like the young guys on the test," and everybody laughed in relief, and we carried on.

Another way of fostering positive relationships between people was to envision interdependence. This was done either by calling attention to interdependence that already existed by naming it or referring to it or, to the extent one's position in the hierarchy allowed, creating material practices that would encourage this kind of behavior.

For example, one engineer who managed the work process for eighteen people, formalized the notion of interdependence as an outcome by creating a category of work she called "interfacing." She describes how and why she included this activity on a subordinate's list of objectives:

The output of Peg's group is very closely tied to customer documentation, so that's why she's the interface to that group. She'll be able to help them the most. And she always knew she was the interface to that group. It was working that way because it made sense, but it wasn't formalized. It wasn't in her objectives anywhere, but I want it to be on her objectives because its a task I want her to do, to value, and to know it's important. . . . So it should be clear that all those things are taking time, and no one had them written down anywhere: We just do it because you've got to. Well, if you've got to, write it down. If it all goes well, that's good. You get "attaboys" for that. You know, when we hear there are no problems with customer documentation? Well, we should be saying, "Good job, Peg!" and "Good job, Dick Roberts!" (documentation person), but we should also be saying, "Good job, Peg! You were a major contributing factor even though you didn't do [the actual documentation]."

This action acknowledges and makes visible the work that goes into connecting, building, and maintaining good working relationships with other members of the group, in the service of the collective. Two engineers who work for her describe how this same manager has created an environment of interdependence where it is seen as a sign of competence, not incompetence, to ask for help:

By saying that somebody is having difficulty or something, there's no judgment made in that statement because nobody is going to have an easy time with everything. And it could just be that your machine isn't working that day. It doesn't mean that you don't know your job. I think a lot of places, if somebody walked in and said to the manager, "Oh, you know, my peer is having problems with this," there would be a judgment implied in that. But in our group there is no judgment implied in that. It's not because Arlene is trying to say that she could have done it better than I could, or anything like that. She's just trying to help out.

Those who were not yet in a position to create structures to support collaboration and interdependence could nonetheless envision for others what that type of structure would look like. In the roundtable, one engineer described an incident that had occurred days ago but was still bothering her. She recounted that although she believes in sharing information to help others, doing it made her feel naïve, as though she had been led "down the garden path":

He asked for help. And by the time we were done, it had taken over an hour, and I was angry that I had spent the time with this person, not because I shouldn't help because I think I should help, but I gave him a significant amount of information that had been accumulated through a lot of effort in my group over six to eight months. So I did him a big favor. But I don't have any trust that I'm going to get anything back for that. Now he has all this information, which is good for the company, but the people that he works with are going to think that, you know, "Oh, wow, look what he knows." And I don't feel that there is any way that comes back to me. So I'm frustrated that I spent the time helping him, and yet when I think about it, should I not have helped him? And made him spend six months [duplicating the work]? It [sharing the information] was the right thing for the company . . . that's got to be right . . . and yet it had a negative impact on me.

Participants identified with this story and were able to recognize the issue as symptomatic of a culture that is not structured to reward collaboration and cooperation:

E2: It all has to do with the culture of the company, what they're looking at. Because if all that stuff were recognized, all this behind-the-scenes stuff, then we wouldn't have this conflict. We would just do what we thought was best for the company, and everyone would think that was great and then we would do well, and everyone would be happy.

E3: If the manager you spoke with was rewarded for having gone to an internal source instead of spending six months and all the resources to redo the same work, as well as you being rewarded for sharing the information that you gathered . . . then both sides would have a reason to say what really happened.

E1: Right, it shouldn't be an either/or. Either he gets rewarded *or* I get rewarded. It should be both of us are doing the appropriate thing for the corporation, so we should both be rewarded. When I'm talking "rewarded" here, I'm talking about pats on the head, or "yes, you're an effective person," not "here's a check for you." *Recognition* is a better word than *reward*. We should both be recognized for behaving appropriately because we both *did*. And yet I feel that I won't get any recognition for anything, and we did over six months' worth of work. And the other guy probably will get recognition for doing an hour's worth of work.

As the discussion continued they were able to envision ways in which this type of collaborative behavior could be encouraged. One engineer suggested that notes of appreciation should go not only to the person who shared information but also to that person's manager. Another had a suggestion for how this type of collaboration could be formalized in a way that used company norms:

I was just thinking. We just went through a big reorganization last fall, and even though it was a lot this way before, we are even more of a numbers-oriented company now. You are always supposed to ask, "Does this make financial sense?" before you make a decision. And maybe if finding a source that's already done some work could be put on, say, a manager's financial statement for a project as a cost savings because they didn't have to spend money to do that again? [It would show] they saved money by getting this information in a less-expensive way. Then maybe the managers could be recognized for recognizing other people . . . and there would be some numbers to back it up.

A more subtle way of envisioning interdependence had to do with working to create an environment in which ideas could be built upon, in which people would be encouraged to connect their way of thinking about a problem with someone else's idea in order to come up with a collective solution. As one engineer put it:

I like to talk about things, explain why I think something, hear about what the other person thinks about something. But I know there are some people who like to negotiate in a state of conflict with voices raised, like, "That's *not* a good idea" instead of "Why do you think that's a good idea?"

Other engineers describe making similar efforts to use collaborative language to create a less confrontational environment:

You can find ways to make suggestions rather than contradictions. If a person were to make a statement that you disagreed with, rather than just out-and-out disagree with them, you find that maybe there is a piece of their statement that you can agree with. So you start there, like, "That's a good point, especially this part. What if we looked at it that way, except a little different?" And I find that just these kinds of behaviors [are helpful] . . . just so you are not confronting the other people so much.

In summary, the activities that characterize this fourth category of relational activity are a blend of attending to the individual—creating growth fostering conditions *within* people—and concern for the collective—creating growth-fostering conditions *between* people. Implicit in these efforts is the belief that individuals have a right to be acknowledged or noticed as unique and that part of what it means to be a good coworker is to do the noticing. In practice, this meant listening to others even when they did not feel like listening and taking others' preferences, situations, and pressures into account when making decisions. Rather than action motivated by strong affect, this behavior appeared to be a strategy based on a belief about the potential benefits of working this way—a belief that being conscious of others' feelings creates team spirit.

Relational theorists would agree that individuals who feel understood, accepted, and appreciated are more likely to be accepting of others, leading to what Jean Baker Miller calls a spiraling dynamic of growth. The result can be the creation of trust, an enlarged sense of commitment to one another, and an increased willingness to see another person's point of view.[13] Theories of the origin of self-esteem also suggest that these attributes contribute to feelings of self-worth and can lead to a group life that is characterized by an increased level of energy and desire for interaction, connection, and collective achievement.

The other set of activities that were intended to enhance group life had to do with creating conditions for growth between people. In practice, this meant engaging in behaviors that recognized, acknowledged, and in some way validated the essentially interdependent nature of individual achievement. Facilitating relationships so that people could interact and potentially enable each other was one part of the equation. The other part was envisioning or creating structures to support and reward collaboration. Together, the willingness to put effort into these activities evidenced a belief that achievement, both individual and collective, depended on connection and that all involved, including the project, would benefit if interdependence were encouraged and rewarded.

The process of balancing individual and communal concerns is often cited as an essential feature of growth-fostering activities. For example, Sara Ruddick notes that the thinking, feeling, and reflecting that mothers do before they take action is associated with the balancing of these two competing interests—to celebrate the uniqueness of the child while simultaneously channeling that unique spirit in ways that are acceptable to the community. Marjorie DeVault speaks in similar terms about the goal of creating family. She describes the ways in which mothers attend to individual preferences, feelings, and circumstances of each family member in creating family meals as a social event, and at the same time they work toward reconciling these different interests to produce a common experience. Others have described this separate/connected tension as one of the paradoxes of group life—that in order to be a fully functional participant in the collective one needs to assert and be appreciated for one's own individuality and personality. This allays the fear of being subsumed by the group. At the same time, however, one needs to act as part of the collective in order to develop the level of interdependence and intimacy that will foster that very same individuality and uniqueness.[14]

Many of the beliefs and the behaviors associated with creating team are similar to those Marjorie DeVault describes as essential to creating a sense of family. She contrasts the practical reality of family as an institution with the social reality, the *experience* of family, and suggests that the set of attributes and qualities that are assumed to occur naturally in these small groups of people who share material and emotional resources is not natural or inevitable but is a constructed reality. The image of this social reality is constructed through the social discourse on family, a changing, evolving ideal of what members should or can expect to feel and experience as members of this entity. The reality of this experience, then, does not occur naturally but is instead created, supported, and maintained by material practices. She focuses on one of these practices, feeding the family, to explicate the intentional and deliberate actions undertaken to create a particular social space within which family can be experienced. While creating team did not include feeding the organization in any concrete way, the intention of creating a communal entity and the experience of group life were quite similar.

Implicit in the effort expended to create this communal entity is the belief that the intangible outcomes that result from these efforts are worth it. These intangible outcomes include such things as cooperation, trust, mutual respect, and affection, as well as attitudes, values, and new ways of thinking about things. What makes the outcomes intangible is that they are embedded in people and social interactions. As Cato Wadel notes, they are invisible as the product of work because they do not fit the conventional definition of outcome—a definition that springs from public-sphere experience. To find individuals in the public sphere who would be willing to expend effort to achieve these outcomes implies that these workers are operating from a different belief system and an expanded definition of outcome.

Expending effort in an organizational environment to create the communal entity "team" implies two interior conditions in the workers: first, an expanded definition of outcome, and second, some basic assumptions and beliefs about the possibility, the desirability, and the potential benefits of creating an environment where these outcomes can be realized.

Time and again, the engineers demonstrated a willingness to produce outcomes embedded in others and a belief in the benefits of working in such an environment. They articulated a vision, and at times created the reality of a work environment built on beliefs about collective growth in connection.

In terms of skills, the behavior in this category required an ability to respond empathetically to others and to understand the emotional context in which others operated. In addition, it required a type of cognitive complexity not dependent on affect, one similar to what Irene Stiver calls "response/ability," which refers to the capacity to freely and wholeheartedly engage with another person's subjectivity, and at the same time maintain and acknowledge one's own subjectivity in order to create something new.[15]

Summary

Relational practice is a way of working that reflects a relational logic of effectiveness and requires a number of relational skills such as empathy, mutuality, reciprocity, and a sensitivity to emotional contexts. From the perspective of the engineers, working this way was strategically motivated. It was intentional behavior, motivated by the belief that this way of working was a more effective way of achieving goals and getting the job done.

In the introduction to this chapter I explained the methodological purpose of describing relational practice from a perspective consistent with its own values and belief system. Telling the story that way—that is, staying within the perspective and value system of the engineers themselves and highlighting the relational skills, strategic intention, and underlying beliefs of the perspective—allows the description to retain its full power as a "subversive story." In other words, it allows the engineers' stories to retain their full power to challenge current organizational assumptions and accepted truths. However, as noted earlier, the goal of telling a subversive story is not to *replace* the truth claims of one discourse with the truth claims of another. Poststructuralists such as Roy Jacques remind us that the goal of such stories is to create a tension "between experience and various ways of representing that experience to show what the

Table 2
Relational Practice

Preserving	Mutual Empowering	Self-Achieving	Creating Team
Focus on Task: *Shouldering responsibility for the whole in order to preserve the life and well-being of the project by:*	**Focus on Other:** *Enacting an expanded definition of "outcome" to include outcomes embedded in others such as increased knowledge or competence by:*	**Focus on Self:** *Using relational skills to enhance one's ability to achieve goals by:*	**Focus on Team:** *Creating background conditions in which group life can flourish and the feeling of team can be experienced by:*
Resolving conflict and disconnection to keep project connected to essential resources	Teaching with an awareness of the learner's needs and barriers	Recognizing and accepting responsibility for breaks in relationships that could impede achievement	Affirming individual uniqueness through listening, respecting, and responding
Anticipating and taking action to prevent problems	Sharing information	Re-connecting after disconnection	Facilitating connections among individuals by absorbing stress, reducing conflict, and creating structural practices that encourage interdependence
Extending job beyond defined boundaries and "doing whatever it takes"	Facilitating connections	Reflecting on one's behavior	
	Supplying relational skills	Using feelings as a source of data to understand and anticipate reactions and consequences	
Extending responsibility beyond the technical definition of the job (up, down, lateral)	Protecting others from consequences of their relational ineptitude	Responding to emotional data (emotional context, others' emotional realities) to understand situations and strategize appropriate responses	
Placing project needs ahead of individual career concerns	Giving help without making receiver feel guilty or inadequate	Asking for help in a way that takes the helper's needs and likely responses into account (relational asking)	
	Eliminating barriers and cutting slack		

Table 3
Relational Skills

Empathic competence: Ability to understand others' experiences and perspectives

Emotional competence: Ability to understand and interpret emotional data and use it to assess situations and strategize appropriate actions or verbal responses

Authenticity: Ability to access and express one's own thoughts and feelings

Fluid expertise: Ability to move easily from expert to non-expert role, with a genuine openness to being influenced by and learning from others. Ability to acknowledge help and give credit to others with no loss of self-esteem

Vulnerability: Ability to admit "not knowing," to seek others help and expertise with no loss of self-esteem

Embedding outcomes: Ability to empower and contribute to the development of others

Holistic thinking: Ability to synthesize thinking, feeling, and acting

Response/ability: Ability to engage with and respond to others while holding on to one's own reality

---

boundaries and limits might be."[16] Creating this tension calls attention to underlying assumptions and creates an opportunity to discuss and question them. Poststructuralists think of this as an act of resistance because it creates "discursive space" in which new things can be said and new ways of thinking can emerge.

This chapter was the first step in creating discursive space where new things might be said and new ways of thinking about work, skill, and competence might emerge. It intentionally tells the story of relational practice *as if* it is the only plausible interpretation of the behavior and *as if* no tension exists between it and the current definition of work in organizational discourse. I asked readers to stay in this poststructuralist paradox by suspending their inclination to interpret the behavior differently and join me in reading it as if it were the only story that could be told.

The next chapter, chapter 5, moves to part two of the analysis. The goal of the second stage of the analysis is to call attention to the tension between the interpretation of the observed activities from a relational

Table 4
Relational Logic of Effectiveness

Workers are responsible for keeping the project connected to resources it needs

Workers are responsible for the whole

Competence will be recognized without self-promotion

Growth, achievement, and effectiveness occur best in a context of connection

Achievement occurs within a network of connection and support

Enabling others requires paying attention to emotional context

Enabling others requires paying attention to intellectual context

Definition of outcome includes outcomes embedded in people

Definition of outcome includes outcomes embedded in social situations

The short term costs of maintaining relationships are an investment in long-term potential for growth/effectiveness

Interdependence is a powerful vs. deficient state

Dependence and independence are fluid (vs. static or achieved) states

Severed relationships are an obstacle to future growth and achievement

Authenticity (acknowledging vulnerability and need as well as strength, skill, and expertise) is a necessary condition for mutual growth-in-connection

---

perspective and those same activities when interpreted through a conventional perspective on work. Although the analysis itself is intended to highlight the tension between the two perspectives, it may relax some of the anxiety readers might have felt in struggling not to make alternative interpretations of the engineers' stories. As noted earlier, a relational belief system—in which relational interactions are assumed to be sites of growth, achievement, and professional effectiveness—stands in contrast to traditional organizational norms and beliefs about competence, effectiveness, and organizational success. Chapter 5 focuses on what happens to this relationally motivated behavior when it is brought into a conventional organizational discourse—one that is hostile to its relational assumptions. It explores how relational practice is understood and interpreted according the "truth rules" of organizational discourse in an engineering work environment.

5

Disappearing Acts: Gender and Power at Work

The previous chapter describes relational practice from within its own discourse, in terms consistent with its own belief system and underlying assumptions. This chapter explores what happens to the same behavior when it is brought into organizational discourse. How is relationally motivated behavior understood and perceived when subjected to the assumptions and logic of effectiveness underlying the definition of work in an engineering environment?

As noted earlier, I had been working on a research team in this firm for over two years before I began work on this study. The cultural diagnosis[1] the team had done as part of that earlier work indicated that this was a highly masculine work environment typical of other organizations in which design engineering was valued.[2] For example, it was a work environment where individual heroics were highly prized. Time and again our research team was told that the way to get ahead was to solve "high-visibility" problems. Solving a problem of this type was referred to as hitting a home run, and we were told that steady contributors, or singles hitters, were not as likely to get promoted as those who stepped forward in critical situations and found solutions to such problems. "Real" work was consistently defined this way. Engineers who moved on to supervisory positions spoke of "no longer having a real job" because they no longer did this type of hands-on problem solving.

It was a work culture that placed a high value on talking about problems regardless of whose responsibility they were. People expressed frustration with meetings where members would talk endlessly about technical problems, even when they did not have the relevant people present or all the information needed to address them. As one female engineer noted about managers who seemed to enjoy technical talk, "I think there's a lot of frustrated engineers running these programs."

What she saw as frustrated engineers having fun talking technical, McIlwee and Robinson suggest is a required manner of demonstrating competence in engineering environments. In their study of engineering cultures, they found that "competence is a function of how well one presents an image of an aggressive, competitive, technically oriented person. The style is as important as its substance." Style includes things like an obvious love, bordering on obsession, of tinkering and a "fascination with and desire to talk at length about these activities."[3]

This eagerness to associate oneself with a high-visibility problem by solving it or talking about it reinforced certain cultural norms about self-promotion, autonomy, and individualism. If only home run hitters are rewarded, it makes little sense to spend time helping others advance bases. Being quietly competent—or contributing indirectly—translated into not being competent at all. To be seen as competent, you needed to verbally or physically demonstrate your ability to "bend your mind" around a problem in order to come up with a unique or previously unheard of solution. This led to something many people called the "not-invented-here" syndrome. The chief engineer was the first person we heard use this term to describe the work culture of the design and manufacturing unit. He said that no one liked to spend time adopting, adapting, or reiterating another person's solution. It was inventing something unique, different, and singularly yours that was considered fun and worthwhile. Anything less was seen as not real engineering. Just as supervisors were seen, not only by others but even in their own view of themselves, as no longer doing real work, so too were engineers who had moved on to marketing or quality control. Technical specialization was clearly the valued commodity; generalists were suspect.

In an environment where solving technical problems was seen as the measure of worth, and a love of tinkering was a measure of one's competence, the definition of output tended to be quite narrow. Output was defined as the result of real work, and that meant something tangible, concrete, measurable, and quantifiable. There was a strong belief that if you cannot define the metrics of something up front, its value cannot be assessed. The focus on tangible output as an indication of real work was reinforced by a belief in what some called a "one best way" approach to doing the work. That is, it was assumed that if a problem were thought about long and hard, one best answer would emerge. Not only did this lead to endless efforts to standardize the work process in order to capture the one right way, it also reinforced the individualistic goal of being the one person identified with having found it.

When behavior motivated by a relational belief system (model of growth-in-connection) was brought into this organizational discourse it *got disappeared* as work because it violated many of the norms mentioned above. In other words, when behavior motivated by a relational or stereotypically feminine logic of effectiveness was brought into this discourse, it got disappeared as work because it violated the masculine logic of effectiveness that was in operation. By re-reading the textual representation of work collected in the shadowing, interviewing, and roundtable discussion, by observing and listening closely to how others responded to those who enacted relational practice, and by noting my own reactions to observing these activities, I was able to identify several aspects of the process by which relational practice got disappeared in this setting.

Disappearing the Practice of Preserving

The practice of preserving is rooted in a belief system that privileges context and connection. As such, it violated many of the underlying assumptions about effectiveness prevalent in this work culture—assumptions based on individualism, independence, and the hierarchical separation of functions. For example, one aspect of preserving behavior had to do with assuming responsibility for the whole. In practice this meant doing "whatever it takes" to ensure the health and well-being of the project even if that meant putting aside one's personal agenda or sacrificing some symbols of status or hierarchy. However, in a culture based on individuation and autonomy, in which technical competence and specialization are privileged, "picking up a soldering iron," passing information across functions, or letting someone else present your data were activities outside the job description.

In fact, the personal payback for these activities seemed to be invisible to others, who often acted mystified by the behavior. For example, the engineer who attempted to pass information across functions by telling her manager that marketing would be sending out substandard prints, was met with a shrug and a dismissive wave of the hand. The manager did not thank her for what she had done or give any verbal or nonverbal affirmation that this was appreciated or expected. The nonverbal message was "that's not your job—don't worry about it." In a work culture where beliefs about what it means to be an effective worker are based on norms of specialization, the willingness to take responsibility for the whole was puzzling. Another engineer who called her boss to warn of a possible duplication of effort was met with a similar response, which suggested such a warning was annoying interference or excessive attention to detail rather than valuable feedback.

In a culture where solving problems is more highly valued than preventing them, it is perhaps no wonder that doing things that prevented confusion was not seen as real work. As one engineer put it, "If nothing [bad] happens, it's assumed it's because nothing was going to happen, which isn't always the case." Thus, picking up the slack—doing things because "if I don't do them, no one will"—was not easy to articulate as an activity that added value to the project.

And, in a work culture where differential reward is based on hierarchy and status, it was difficult to advocate that doing low-status work, like picking up a soldering iron, was a good strategy. On the contrary, the engineers were well aware that in this work culture doing low-status work was not seen as a sign of competence, but rather as a sign of career naïveté. They might recognize the value it added and even wish others would work this way. But they also knew how this behavior would be interpreted by others, and they cautioned each other not to do too much of it. In the roundtable discussion one engineer takes on the voice of the dominant discourse and reminds engineers of the likely consequences of doing lower-status work.

I very much agree with the fundamental statement that no one should feel above doing any of the pieces of the task that need to be done to get the task done. And this is rampant around here, that attitude of "I'm too good for this; I'm paid too much to do this." But on the other hand, you can get into a problem. If all the technicians are supporting other engineers [who won't pick up a soldering iron], then you will be saddled with both the technical and the engineering work. So with having a good attitude, you can get yourself taken advantage of . . . if you are not careful.

She notes that in this work culture, having "a good attitude" gets interpreted as a willingness to be exploited. If you do it, you will not get the technical support you need but will be expected to do everything yourself. Although many in the roundtable nodded in agreement at this statement, the ambivalence they felt about the interpretation is brought into the discussion by others who challenged this way of thinking and offered an alternative:

Well, I've found that because I'm willing to pick up the soldering iron, technicians are ten times more willing to do work that I ask them to do. I've had technicians say things to me, like . . . a technician I don't know will walk into the lab, and I'll be talking to a technician I know, and the other new guy that I don't know will be quiet. And the other one will say, "That's OK, she's not like the rest of them." And I get lots more help because I don't feel like I'm better than they are.

Other members of the roundtable agree that this has been their experience, even though it seems to contradict accepted wisdom. One notes,

I come into the lab and say [to the technician], "Oh, you're busy." And they say, "No, I've got time to do that for you." And they take it.

Another agrees:

Or, they'll say, "Why don't you go work on that other thing? I'll do this for you." They volunteer to take some of your tasks. But, I'll tell you, the other people? The people who do the other stuff? No way. Those are the ones who when they come in with stuff to get done, the technicians will say, "Well, I'm doing this for this person and that for that person, but I might be able to fit you in next Wednesday." You know?

This series of quotes suggests how difficult it is to offer an alternative interpretation of behavior that would challenge conventional wisdom. Is working this way good for the project, and does it enhance your own effectiveness? Or does it make you a chump being exploited by others? The engineers vacillate between these two interpretations, uncomfortable in both domains.

Although this engineering environment was particularly masculine, it is probable that preserving activities would fare no better in other work cultures. Certainly, conventional wisdom warns women away from this kind of behavior. Rather than being seen as evidence of taking responsibility for the whole, it is often portrayed in popular how-to books for women managers as just the opposite—that is, a tendency to focus on minutiae or an excessive devotion to duty.[4] In fact, I found that even I, as an observer who was making an effort to view the engineers' behavior through a relational lens, "disappeared" this type of competence, interpreting it instead as a personal weakness. When I observed the event described earlier of an engineer who took a back seat in a meeting and let her boss talk about her data, I first coded this as evidence of her fear of power and success. I wrote the word "meek" in the margins of my notes. I made sense of her behavior as a type of personal inadequacy and assumed that she was uncomfortable with self-promotion or with being seen as an expert. It was not until later, when she spoke of the incident with pride and explained it was an intentional strategy on her part to give the problem increased visibility and make sure it was taken seriously, did I realize her behavior at that meeting could be understood differently. Only then did I realize that I had "disappeared" her work by labeling the behavior as inappropriate to the workplace and as evidence of her personal inadequacy.

The type of disappearing I did as a researcher could have taken many forms. For example, readers or observers who were focused on gender dynamics at work might have seen some aspects of preserving behavior, like sending thank-you notes, as wives' work and might have attributed it to women's desire to humanize the workplace.[5] Others might have noted the caring for individuals inherent in trying to give others the information they need to prepare for a meeting and have attributed it to an ethic of care. Still others might have stereotyped the behavior and seen it as further evidence that men focus on task and women focus on process. While each of these interpretations might represent some aspect of the experience, all of them fall short of capturing the essence of the behavior as the engineers themselves describe it. That is, all of these conventional explanations are fundamentally different from describing the practice as work—strategic action—intended to keep the project connected to outside resources.

Disappearing the Practice of Mutual Empowering

The practice of mutual empowering also violated some important assumptions and traditional rules for success in the organizational discourse. In a culture of independence and self-promotion—where individual achievement is prized and competition means beating the other guy and finishing on top—voluntarily helping others achieve is deviant behavior. Indeed, enacting a relational belief system in which interdependence is a natural state and enabling others is a source of self-esteem so violated professional norms that it seemed that the easiest way to make sense of the behavior was to attribute it to powerlessness or naïveté.

These attributions were confirmed by an organizational system that did in fact take advantage of those who were helpful. In the roundtable, an engineer spoke of a coworker who, because he was in a supporting role, was getting worried that he would be a "gopher" forever:

I'm just working in this new group, and there's this guy who is starting to be another [quality expert]. But he will do it . . . he'll do everything. He'll pack up Joe's stuff because Joe is too high up to do it, you know? So I know this guy will really get things done. So I go to him all the time and it's kind of—. . . . I've heard him express a little bit of concern that he likes to do this kind of stuff, that he likes to be helpful . . . and he's really got a very good attitude for a guy [group laughs]. . . . But he is to the point where he is expressing a little concern that he does have a higher mission in life.

In an environment where helping others achieve goals "gets disappeared" as valuable work (those who get paid to do it, such as secretaries and other support staff, are considered no more than "gophers"), it makes sense that those who voluntarily assume this role are considered either incapable of achieving in their own right or too naïve to know better. Either explanation devalues the activity itself. Giving help is not seen as work. It is not understood as the product or output of someone's effort, but as the product of someone's inadequacy. As one engineer comments:

If you try to nurture, they just don't get it. They don't understand that is what you are doing. They see it as a weakness, and they use it against you. They don't see that you are doing it consciously. . . . They think you have missed something or that they've gotten something over on you. So if you try to be nice, you end up doing other people's work. I've gotten so that now I say, "OK, look, I'll help you out on this one. *But you owe me one.*"

Her experience suggests that in this environment, if you put effort into achieving outcomes that are embedded in others you are likely to be seen *not* as someone working in a way that enhances organizational learning and effectiveness, but rather as someone who is weak, naïve, or exploitable. Her language is revealing. She rejects the negative attribution of "weakness" that she feels others might use to describe her willingness to help out. She tries to find stronger, more accurate descriptors of the behavior. However, the words and phrases available to her end up reinforcing rather than challenging this negative attribution. Phrases like "being nice" and "try to nurture" de-skill the practice, making it seem more like evidence of a personal attribute than conscious, intentional action. She resolves the dilemma and resists the disappearing of her intentional action by saying "you owe me one," making it clear that helping is something everyone, not just nice people, can do.

The norm of ignoring or discounting help and the practice of taking full credit for collective achievements run deep and are reinforced by routine interactions. Recall the engineer who helped someone from another group by giving him the results of six months of her team's work and now felt in conflict, as if she had been "led down the garden path." Her dilemma indicates that she was well aware of how the myth of independence disappears enabling activity. She is also aware of what things would have to change to dislodge this myth and replace it with the reality of interdependence:

If we rewarded someone who said, "You know that action item I got yesterday? I found this great source of information [within the company]. So and so's team did all this work, and here is some of the output." And if [the boss] could say, "That was good of you to not reinvent the wheel," and you could actually get recognized for the *way* you got the job done rather than just getting it done. Just getting it done is what is important here . . . so you alone . . . *you're* the one who got it done . . . so you alone get the credit.

During the roundtable discussion she was given suggestions on how to make her help more visible but she rejects them because they do not meet her standard of collaborative behavior. For example, she rejects the suggestion that she could simply have told him she was worried that her team would not get credit for their work:

No, no, [I don't want to do that] because then all I would feel like I was doing was telling him he shouldn't come and ask [for help]. And I did feel he was behaving appropriately by not trying to reinvent the wheel. So I support that process, which is not always followed around here. So on the one hand I was saying, "Oh, this is good that he came in and asked the question" but "this is bad that I have to spend an hour doing this, and now he's going to look good, and I don't think he should look as good as he's going to look." But then I feel bad . . . that I shouldn't feel that way.

It seems she would prefer to keep the enabling invisible in the interaction but assumed in the result. That is, she wants her team to be recognized but she does not want to ask for the recognition. Instead, she wants a work environment where interdependence and mutual empowerment are routine behavior and where enabling and being enabled are recognized as signs of competence. In her view, only in an environment where being enabled was rewarded—where a boss would say, "That was good of you to not reinvent the wheel"—could enabling behavior be truly valued.

For those operating from a relational belief system, enabling others was a powerful act, one that brought enhanced self-esteem, a feeling of power, and an opportunity for growth. It met their own internal definition of competence, even though it was not listed on any formal or informal appraisals of performance. As this engineer notes:

I *like* helping people, even though it's not on my performance appraisal. It's an informal network here, and I know that I can go to them for help someday. It's fun to help someone out, explain to them what you are doing and why, so they can fix it themselves next time.

Another goes beyond describing it as something she likes to do and tries to redefine it as part of what it means to do a good job:

I know I am doing a good job when people think of me, when they have a problem. I've succeeded when people think of me as someone who is (1) competent and (2) someone who will help. Most people around here only care about the first thing—competence—they don't care if they are seen as approachable. I do.

This quote is a good example of how the ability to describe enabling as a powerful activity is limited by language. She tries to expand the definition of competence, or doing a good job, to include a willingness and an ability to share and empower others. But it is difficult. No organizationally strong words come to mind to describe this aspect of work. In an organizational context, competence would result in some sort of bottom-line outcome. But she wants to call attention to a different kind of outcome, one embedded in another person. And this does not fit the organizational definition of outcome as measurable, quantifiable, and tangible. She decides to break the definition of doing a good job into two parts. One, the technical part of the job, she calls competence, and the second, she calls approachability and a willingness to help. The problem is that the words she has available to describe the nontechnical part of the job, approachability and willingness to help, are not only organizationally weak but also leave the definition of competence unchallenged. In fact, the language and oppositional sentence structure she chooses actually *reinforce* the notion that enabling others is not part of competence but is something separate, the "soft side" of doing a good job. Her effort to challenge the organizational definitions of real work and good workers falls short of the mark.

Disappearing the Practice of Self-Achieving

In this engineering work culture, where models of growth and achievement are based on individuation, independence, and autonomy, those seeking growth and achievement through connection, stood *outside* the discourse on achievement. Their behavior violated norms and was at odds with accepted organizational narratives about success and effectiveness. They were, in other words, destined to be misunderstood. Engineers who put effort into connecting, reconnecting, and maintaining relationships in the service of their own achievement often felt they were in danger of being seen as people who need to be liked. They worried they would be perceived as seeking affection rather than seeking effectiveness and enhanced achievement.

They had good reason to worry. As the following quote indicates, it is difficult to articulate the possibility that achievement needs might be met through relational means. Indeed, in trying to transcend the achievement/affiliation dichotomy, this engineer ends up going around in circles, contradicting herself several times:

So if I do get into a situation that is confrontational, not angry necessarily, but even if we're just being very direct with each other and this person wants to do it one way and I want to do it another way, I'd be concentrating more on [pauses, then laughs a little] *winning* than on how they felt about it. I gave up a long time ago caring about how they felt about it, other than if how they feel about it is going to get in the way of getting it done. But if I don't perceive that their feelings are going to get in the way, then I kind of don't notice anymore [laughs]. So that's the only reason why I'm paying attention to their feelings. It isn't that I care that much about their feelings. It's because if they feel threatened enough, I won't make any progress and not because—. . . . If I thought I'd win in spite of that, it wouldn't bother me at all. So it isn't that I'm terribly worried about whether the guys that I work with *like* me. I worry a lot about whether they respect me. *I don't really care if they like me or not* [emphasis added]. [Laughs.] . . . I happen to think that usually those kind of end up going together, though. If you respect someone, you usually end up liking them, too, at the end of it all.

The contradictions and inconsistencies in this quote give a good sense of what happens when relational practice is brought into the organizational discourse on work. The engineer struggles for language to represent her experience. In doing so, she is careful to distance herself from the interpretation that she is acting inappropriately by paying attention to feelings. She would be more concerned about winning, she wants me to know, than she would about someone's feelings. But then she becomes entangled as she tries to describe her experience and belief that these two things are not mutually exclusive. If feelings were going to get in the way of success, she notes, then of course she would be concerned about them. On the other hand, if feelings were not real, that is if she accepted the conventional wisdom that feelings are irrelevant to organizational phenomena, she would not care about them at all because they would not stand in the way of winning. So, she struggles to make it clear that although she might pay attention to feelings, the reason she would be concerned about others' feelings is not because she wants to be liked. She understands that this would be the obvious attribution, and she wants to make sure I do not make it regarding her. In her effort, she falls into drawing the conventional dichotomy—she would not care if they liked her as long as they respected her. Any language available to her to describe worrying about the effect of confrontation on the relationship, or to describe the possibility that behavior that gets you liked might also make you more effective, would risk the attribution of needing to be liked, an attribution that would taint her as weak or even incompetent. Not having language to describe such a possibility and still be considered competent, she chooses to represent herself as competent. This reinforces rather than challenges the dichotomy, but it serves her purpose of signaling that she is savvy enough to understand the difference between being liked versus being respected. However, after giving me the party line, she recognizes the inadequacy of what she has said in trying to capture her experience. After a slight pause and a little laugh, she undermines her own dichotomous thinking and says these two things "kind of end up going together," that being liked and being respected are not mutually exclusive.

Others went through similar verbal gymnastics to simultaneously resist and comply with the dominant discourse and its conventional definitions of appropriate ways of working. For example, this engineer gives voice to organizational assumptions about the necessary separation of work life from personal life. She carefully aligns herself with the normative belief that you are one person at work and another at home:

I was talking to this guy the other day about it. And I said that you really have to be two totally different people: a business person who is really direct and then at home a different personality. So at home sometimes I just withdraw, and they don't understand. And he said, "Would you write that down and send it to my wife?" [Laughs.]

After a little pause, she continues, subtly undermining this home/work dichotomy by offering an alternative in which the same rules apply in both settings, even though conventional wisdom suggests otherwise:

But, really, I don't think . . . I think confrontation doesn't really work that well in the business place. Like all that women's lib stuff about demanding what you need? It doesn't work that way.

One way of representing the avoidance of confrontation as an effective way of working without seriously challenging the dominant definition of real work, is to attribute it to personal style. Engineers used this attribution often, introducing their description of an alternative way of working by saying things like, "at least for me personally," or "it's just a style thing," or "I'm just more comfortable when. . . ." Using individual differences to explain their preferences almost—but not quite—disappears this way of working as a serious challenge to the norm. As these engineers noted in the roundtable discussion:

E1:   Raised voices are not uncommon. It depends on who you work with and what . . . and we've talked about this—I've talked to several different people here about these things before. But it constantly amazes me, and I really think this is in large part a male thing, how men can be in a room, they'll be in a meeting, at each other's throats, hurling personal insults at each other, and then the meeting is over, and they are like, "Hey, where do you want to go for lunch?" Boom, over, that's it. It was part of the meeting, now the meeting is over, and it's gone. To me, being that angry is a personal thing, and I can't just let it go at the end of the meeting. I'm mad for hours after that happens.

E2:   I don't want to eat lunch with them [group laughs].

E3:   I don't want to each lunch *at all.*

E1:   I just can't let it go. I wish I could. I mean I don't think it is great to be yelling and screaming, but if you're going to do it, I think it's great to be able to just let it go. But I can't do that. That's why I don't like to use it as a tool. But I think that's why a lot of men can use that because it's a tool, it's not an emotion, it's just a tool.

E4:   Then you put it down and go home.

E3:   It's a surface thing, it doesn't really—it's not coming from inside. It's just, "OK, I think I'll make my point with a loud voice."

Within the confines of organizational discourse, they struggle to reevaluate their inability to divorce themselves from the relational, long-term effects of an angry exchange. They reframe the issue, claiming that they worry about the relational not because their relationships with others would be damaged, but because they have a different personal style. This attribution is less damaging than being labeled as someone who needs to be liked, but it, too, has a downside. Having a different style is perilously close to being inappropriate, a point that becomes obvious as they voice the concern that maybe personal style is really personal weakness. They wish they did not take things so personally. But once again, this definition of relational behavior as an aberration or weakness does not fit their experience. A little later in the discussion they expressed this ambivalence and a challenge to the dominant discourse surfaces:

Actually, I'm not sure confrontation is effective for the long term. It's effective right at the instant. But if you're not a team player and *people don't like working with you* [emphasis added], you're not going to be effective in the long run. So it's not good for you. So there's this short term "yes, I can stop what's going on in this meeting. I can have an impact. We can make progress today." But three months from now nobody is even going to let me into the room because I'm so disruptive to the meetings that they aren't getting stuff done.

This quote challenges the organizational discourse and its assumption that conflict and confrontation are tools to be used. The engineer offers an alternative reality. Maybe these angry interactions are not tools that could be used and then forgotten, maybe they *do* have some long-term effect on the relationship between the parties and some long-term effect on the project. This challenge to the discourse—although weakened and constrained by the language available to represent it—nonetheless opens up the possibility that alternative ways of increasing one's own achievement exist: Maybe acting in ways that result in people liking you is a sign of long-term effectiveness.

Disappearing the Practice of Creating Team

The practice of creating team "got disappeared" through a similar process. Despite some organizational rhetoric about teamwork and collaboration, this was a work culture in which individual heroism was highly valued. Thus, it was understandably difficult to articulate or understand the motivation to engage in activity intended to enhance group life or collective achievement. For example, this engineer had difficulty describing her effort to use collaborative language to create an environment where ideas could be explored rather than attacked. She notes that if you use this approach, rather than being seen as effective, you and your ideas disappear. In the roundtable discussion, she described this disappearing so vividly that the group laughed in recognition:

Sometimes if you're in a meeting, and somebody states an idea—if I stand up and I say, "That's totally inappropriate, that's just plain stupid; this is what we should do," or if I stand up and say, "Well, that's a really good idea but another way of looking at it is this. . . ." The person who stood up and was abusive about it is the person that people are going to remember as having come up with that idea later, when it's time to evaluate people. [This last sentence is said quite forcefully, and then after a slight pause and in a softer, more tentative voice, she adds:] I think, lots of times. [Back to a more forceful tone, she continues:] Because even though it's a bad impression, you've made an impression. The other person, in being polite and a little self-effacing, has sort of melted into the background. Sometimes, if you're nice, you'll say— . . . I might be in a meeting and somebody will come up with an idea, and I'll say, "Well, that's a really good idea, but I looked at it this way and this is what I came up with." And then [after you give your idea] they'll say, "Well, anyways . . ." [group laughs]. And because you haven't, like, stomped on them, *you're not even in the room.*

She calls attention to something others have obviously experienced: If there is only one right way, and discovering it makes you the winner, then building on others' ideas is likely to be considered inappropriate, or a sign that you have nothing new to add. Again, the private-sphere language she uses to describe the behavior—nice, polite, self-effacing—are words that de-skill and devalue it. This contributes to its near invisibility as a challenge to confrontational norms. Not having organizationally strong language available to describe nonconfrontational behavior, she uses words that associate it with femininity (polite, nice) and powerlessness (self-effacing). This belies her belief in it as a strategy that could make visible the reality of creating teamwork, by, for example, creating a shared solution to a problem that might transcend any one individual's ideas. This relational belief about how people learn and how creative ideas are born is buried in her description of her own personal style:

> I see it as avoiding conflict. Because at least for me personally, I'm not somebody who feels very comfortable negotiating in an atmosphere of conflict. *I like to talk about things, explain why I think something, hear about what the other person thinks about something* [emphasis added]. But I know that there are some people that— . . . They like to negotiate in a state of conflict with voices raised, like, "That's *not* a good idea" instead of "Why do you think that's a good idea?" So if I can keep it from ever getting elevated to that, then I can be working in an atmosphere that is more comfortable for me. I don't like yelling and screaming and accusations and the rest of that stuff.

Summary: Disappearing Acts

This description of the way each type of relational practice was brought into the discourse suggests that there is a dynamic process involved in which relational practice "gets disappeared" as work and gets constructed as something other than work. Three separate acts of disappearing are evident in the data: The misattribution of motive, the limits of language, and the social construction of gender.

Misattribution of Motive

The first disappearing act is a misinterpretation of the intention underlying relational practice where it is seen as having been motivated not by a desire to work more effectively but by a personal idiosyncrasy or trait. These personal traits included negative characteristics such as naïveté, powerlessness, weakness, and emotional need, as well as more positive attributes such as thoughtfulness, personal style, or being nice.

Table 5
Disappearing Acts

Misinterpreting the intention:

Assuming relational practice is motivated by affect (a need to be liked, emotional dependence) rather than a desire for effectiveness/growth/enhanced achievement

Assuming relational practice is an expression of personal attributes (nice, thoughtful, naïve) or idiosyncrasies (self-deprecating, self-effacing, fearful of confrontation) rather than intentional use of relational skills and abilities

Limits of language:

Organizationally strong words (competence, skill, knowledge) already are defined to exclude relational attributes

Common descriptors of relational attributes (nurturing, empathy, caring) are associated with femininity and are therefore assumed inappropriate to the workplace

Social construction of gender:

Relational behavior is easily conflated with images of "ideal" womanhood and coded as "feminine"

Behavior coded as feminine is devalued in workplace settings

Female engineers are simultaneously *expected to* and *devalued for* acting relationally

---

There are several important characteristics of relational practice that get lost when it is interpreted as a sign of a personal characteristic or aberration. Most notably, the *strategic intention* of the behavior—the attempt to put into practice a different model of effectiveness—is lost. Relational practice is intentional action motivated by a the belief that working this way is better for the project or more effective in getting the job done. From the engineer's perspective, sending notes of appreciation was motivated not by a desire to be thoughtful but by a desire to keep the project connected to the resources it needed to survive. Taking a back seat in a meeting was not an expression of powerlessness but an intentional strategy to give a problem visibility. Using collaborative language was motivated not by a desire to be liked but by a desire to hear and perhaps be influenced by other ideas.

Misinterpreting the motive underlying relational practice makes it difficult to think of the behavior as work. Not only does it disappear the strategic objectives of the practice but also the relational skills needed to enact it. For example, the skill in being able to hold on to one's own idea while actively engaging with others to see what they might have to offer gets lost when the behavior is described as a personal characteristic such as "being polite" or "self-effacing." The intelligence in understanding the emotional context of a teaching interaction and creating the condition where learning can occur is obscured when the behavior is described as thoughtfulness or sensitivity.

Understanding the motivation behind relational practice from the perspective of those who did it, however, raises once again the poststructuralist issue of experience and interpretation. As noted earlier, understanding how a subversive story is disappeared by dominant understandings is different from claiming that the story is an unqualified or transcendent truth. In describing the disappearing dynamic, no claim is being made about which interpretation of behavior is more true. Certainly, intention is not effect. Was the engineer who alerted her manager to the substandard prints being responsible or a nit-picking busybody? Was the engineer who helped someone from another unit a hero or a chump? Was the intentional strategy to enhance effectiveness through relational practice ever realized? This study did not gather data that can answer these questions. Indeed, from the study's poststructuralist perspective, these questions are beside the point. The significant finding is that misinterpreting the motive underlying relational practice taints the behavior as inappropriate and implicitly marks it as "nonwork." This silences the challenge relational practice might present to organizational assumptions about achievement, success, and effectiveness.

In poststructuralist terms, this misattribution of motive fills in the discursive space that might be created by acknowledging a different definition of work based on a model of growth-in-connection. This, in turn, truncates the possibility of theorizing or envisioning alternative, relational strategies for success that might be better or more effective than current practice. It leaves the masculine logic of effectiveness unchallenged. The reason to explore aspects of the disappearing dynamic in such detail is to understand how this silencing occurs. The question of interest is not what is true, but rather, what mechanisms are used to silence challenges to the dominant discourse and how might these mechanisms be resisted so that new ways of working might be considered?

Limits of Language

Language is the second mechanism that silences the challenge relational practice might present to the dominant discourse on work. Many of the words the engineers—and others—used to describe relational practice (helping, nurturing, nice, polite) associated it with the private sphere and femininity. This association genders the behavior, diminishing its organizational relevance and its ability to be perceived as work. Why, you might ask, did the engineers use language that associated their behavior with femininity? As participants in the organizational discourse, they had few options. Creating organizationally strong descriptors of relational behavior is not easy. Words that might have captured the unique belief system underlying their behavior—words like "outcome" and "competence"— are already defined in organizational discourse in ways that implicitly exclude relational aspects of work. For example, the engineers had no way to describe the output of relational activity as an achievement in its own right because outcomes embedded in people, such as confidence, skills, or knowledge, do not fit the conventional definition of outcome as something tangible, measurable, and quantifiable. There is no easy way of talking about embedded outcomes as achievements in their own right, or as the product of intentional action. With no possibility of identifying a "real" outcome, it becomes quite difficult to describe practices such as creating the experience of team or enabling others as "real" work. The engineer who shared her team's solutions with another unit was not seen as doing real work—she was seen as helping out, an activity so atypical and inappropriate that she felt she had been led "down the garden path." Even when enabling others was part of the job, it was difficult to describe in terms of outcomes. As one engineering supervisor noted: "I don't do a lot of real work now. I do a lot of helping people understand what the problem is, helping people believe they can do something on their own."

What further complicates the situation is that words such as skill, intelligence, or outcome—words that have been defined in ways that exclude the relational—are routinely used to operationalize other key organizational concepts such as achievement and self-efficacy. For example, achievement is demonstrated by the attainment of tangible outcomes. In turn, self-efficacy is assumed to be enhanced by experiences in which one can demonstrate this type of achievement and thereby enhance one's individuated sense of self. The effects of language are thus compounded, making it difficult to describe something that lies outside this self-reinforcing framework. Describing the experience of mutual empowerment, i.e., the experience of enhancing one's self-esteem and self-efficacy through increasing one's *interacting* sense of self (rather than one's individuated sense of self), is nearly impossible. Engineers who tried to describe this type of self-efficacy had to resort to saying, for example, that they "liked" helping.

The role language plays in disappearing relational practice highlights the circular nature of the dynamic as well as the methodological issue of listening to women's voice to understand experience. Since this "experience" does not exist outside current gender/power relationships, the only language available to describe it is language that has been created to sustain a status quo in which relational activity is devalued. Thus, the use of relational language to describe the behavior not only "disappears" the organizational relevance of the experience (and with it any challenge to the status quo), but, ironically, reinforces the very interpretation it was seeking to challenge. For example, the engineer who tried to describe a new definition of competence ended up reinforcing the notion that approachability is not competence. Describing the use of collaborative language to build on others' ideas as "being polite" or the practice of maintaining important relationships as "being nice" reinforced the behavior as inappropriate in an engineering work culture rather than challenging this belief.

Social Construction of Gender

The third aspect of the disappearing dynamic relates to the social construction of gender. It is different from the first two aspects of "getting disappeared" because it has to do with how this way of working gets conflated with images of femininity and motherhood. The first two acts of disappearing—the misinterpretation of the motive and the effects of language—would probably be a factor for anyone who works this way, regardless of gender. But when women enact relational practice, something else happens and a gender dynamic kicks in.

Because of gender roles, the female engineers felt they were expected to act relationally, to be soft, feminine, helpful, good listeners. In fact, they did not seem to believe they had the option of acting any other way. As one said, "I try swearing, but I feel so stupid!" Another described what happened when she tried using confrontation to make a point:

People notice that you said it, and it definitely gets the point on the table. But it certainly isn't good for your long-term relationships with that person. Especially, I think, if it comes from a woman to a man. I think that another man could do that, could say the exact same words, the exact same tone, and after the meeting it would just be over. . . . I don't think it would be over if one of those players were a woman, even if it were over for the woman. I don't think it would be over for the man.

But being expected to act relationally was only one side of the gender dynamic. The other had to do with being devalued for doing it. As noted earlier, the organizational discourse on work privileges a model of growth and development based on individuation, autonomy, and separation. When faced with behavior symptomatic of a relational model of growth, the system tended to understand it as the devalued side of its own model, i.e., the devalued side of the public/private split. This understanding required an explanation of what might motivate someone to engage in activity that was inherently less valuable and therefore devalued the people who do it. The ready explanation, again rooted in the ideology of true womanhood, was that women have greater emotional dependency needs. In other words, they "want" to do these things and will do them willingly because they motivated by "higher" (i.e., lower) goals. That is, they are somehow "better" than others—they are caring, polite, nice people (sometimes even called saints or angels). This characterization, although seemingly positive, carries within it the implicit assumption that one has to be somehow not living in the real world to engage in this type of behavior willingly. Thus, the language used to describe relational behavior tends to characterize it as a manifestation of this interior craziness, i.e., as emotional or psychological pathology.[6] The engineers experienced this as an attribute of "needing to be liked" or of taking things too personally.

The conflation of gender expectations with relational practice is a powerful way of disappearing the motivation behind the behavior. It was difficult to articulate a relational way of working as an intentional choice when the engineers sensed that they did not *have* a choice. It was difficult not to resent being expected to act relationally and then being devalued or exploited for having acted that way. As a result, the engineers often contradicted themselves or got hopelessly confused as they tried to capture the experience that they simultaneously resented being forced to use relational strategies *and* they believed these strategies were more effective.

Even more problematic, many of the behaviors associated with working relationally are easily conflated with images of femininity and ideal womanhood and can be interpreted as natural expressions of (female) gender. The belief system underlying relational practice gets disappeared in this conflation. The ideology of true womanhood invokes images of women as caregivers and non-women as care receivers. In practice, this attribution of relational activity as something women are, not something they do, disappears the material practice associated with what they do. It also disappears any responsibility for reciprocity: If this practice springs from who one *is*, then one who *is not* has no obligation to respond in kind. When these female engineers provided activity commonly thought of as a natural expression of their gender (e.g., helping, listening, teaching) they unwittingly reinforced a notion of entitlement that is one of the foundations of patriarchy, i.e., women's role in life is to support, and men's is to draw on this support in order to act.

As a result, when female engineers tried to enact mutual empowering, a practice characterized by mutuality and an expectation of reciprocity, they often were misinterpreted as enacting mothering, a practice characterized by selfless giving and no expectation of reciprocity. In other words, they were responded to as *women* within a patriarchal system of power and entitlement, not as peers or coworkers in an organizational hierarchy. They resisted this role. Although they might have been willing to "do whatever it takes" to preserve the life and well-being of an inanimate object such as the project (with no expectation of reciprocal attention), it was clear they were not willing to be cast in this role permanently in their relationships with others. For example, several of the female engineers described routinely being asked to do support tasks by male engineers, such as copying, delivering papers to another office, or packing boxes. When they began to feel the lack of reciprocity and recognized that they were being taken advantage of, they would try to set some boundary around how much or what kind of help they were willing to give. As one said, "I mean, really . . . you can't always give somebody your work. It's OK to do it once in a while—that is not a problem. But you can't *always* do that." When this engineer tried to limit her helping, however, she described being (jokingly) called "Tarantula Lady" or "Queen Bee." Getting called names for not being willing to help limitlessly makes visible the expectation that she, as a woman, should embrace this kind of helping behavior and do it willingly and gladly, with no expectation of reciprocity. To set limits, qualify, or differentiate among different types of help one was willing to give, is to be called not *unhelpful* but *unfeminine*, poisonous, arrogant.

Negative experiences like this overwhelmed the engineers' belief in an alternative way of working. Because they recognized the career implications of being exploited or seen as naïve, they ended up simultaneously touting the value of working this way and cautioning themselves and others not to do too much of it. As one said, "Although it might be good for the project, if you do it, you'll end up being a 'gopher' your whole life."

These aspects of the disappearing dynamic operate in concert, reinforcing and intensifying each other's effects (see Figure 1). The result of these synergistic effects is that activity springing from a relational belief system "gets disappeared" as relational practice (something new) and gets constructed as something familiar (e.g., personal style, a natural expression of gender, private-sphere behavior inappropriate to the public sphere). This sets in motion a misunderstanding of the motivation underlying the behavior that silences its potential challenge to the dominant organizational discourse on work. The disappearing dynamic is a self-reinforcing cycle in which the behavior and its potential benefits are absorbed by the system, but the system itself is not challenged. The female engineers, as participants in the larger system, were themselves caught up in this cycle, wanting to work differently, unwittingly colluding in the disappearing of the behavior as work in the way they talked about it, cautioning each

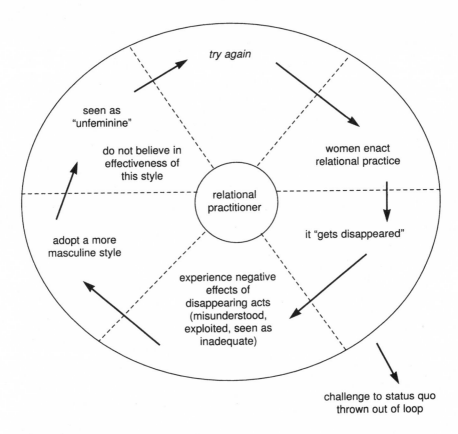

Figure 1
The disappearing dynamic

other about the negative effects of working this way and yet unwilling to give up trying to enact this different, more relational way of working.

The two, contradictory sides of the social construction of gender the engineers experience—being expected and even relied upon to enact relational practice, while being dismissed or devalued for acting that way—embody a more general contradiction that plays itself out in our larger societal systems. Indeed, it is a contradiction inherent in the public/private split that the power-knowledge system of patriarchy works to suppress: *relational activity is not needed and women must provide it.* The implications—and possibility of resisting—this suppressed contradiction are important and will be discussed in chapter 6. For now, the point is that the social construction of gender is a dynamic that suppresses a contradiction inherent in the dominant discourse, a contradiction that must be suppressed for the current power structure between the sexes to continue undisturbed. Thus, the "act of resistance" inherent in opening up discursive space in which new ways of organizing might emerge is not simply an act of resistance to hierarchy or other aspects of organizing. At a deeper level it is an act of resistance to the way in which these ways of organizing create, re-create and maintain an unquestioned acceptance of the separation of the public and private spheres of life and the gender/power structure that depends on this separation.

6

Getting beyond Disappearing

Since this study was completed, I have talked with many women—and some men—about the practical implications of the disappearing dynamic. The stories of "getting disappeared" abound. People such as the scientists, technicians, and analysts we met in the introduction are puzzled by the gap they experience between organizational rhetoric and reality. This chapter explores that gap, why it is more complicated than it first appears, what gender has to do with it, and, finally, what strategies organizations and the people in them—particularly women—are using to get beyond disappearing.

The New Organization

There are strong forces for change in today's globally competitive, knowledge-intensive business environment. Increasingly organizations are being encouraged—even warned—to reinvent themselves, push decision making to lower levels, encourage teamwork and collaboration, flatten the hierarchy, and think systemically. These new organizational forms will need new kinds of workers. A few years ago, Michael Hammer and James Champy described this new employee in their influential book, *Reengineering the Corporation,* as someone who must accept ownership of problems, work in a team and engage in continuous learning as part of the job.[1] Today, the call for such changes in workers has intensified. Organizations are being exhorted in increasingly stronger terms to adopt new models of success and develop new skills in their workers.[2]

Many aspects of relational practice fit this new image of empowered workers who not only take responsibility for their work and their own learning but accept a more general responsibility for the whole. In fact, relational practice includes many functions that traditionally have been reserved for managers. Distributing these functions—such as enabling and developing others, thinking systemically, anticipating consequences, and connecting across functions—and generalizing them to the entire population could go a long way to making the new organization a reality. The problem is that these practices depend on skills and competencies not commonly associated with routine everyday effectiveness in the way one works. Skills such as paying attention to emotional data, sensitivity to others' emotional realities, self-reflection, and "fluid expertise" are not typically included in developmental programs or training sessions. The issue is that these practices depend on skills—and, even more significant, a whole way of seeing and interacting with others—that are an integration of values commonly associated with the public work sphere and those commonly associated with the private, family sphere. This suggests that if organizations want to develop relational practitioners, their reward systems, structures, work practices, and norms must change. These systems will need to reflect a new reality, a new set of skills, and new ways of treating others that are an integration of traits and practices commonly associated with masculine domains (technical competence, autonomous action, competitiveness, and linear thinking) and those associated with feminine domains (empathy, enabling, collaboration, trust).

The Challenge: Simple but Not Easy

While the connections between relational practice and the new organization seem obvious and the implications straightforward, the findings suggest that taking relational practice seriously may not be so easy. Indeed, the disappearing dynamic helps us to understand why relational practitioners often feel disheartened rather than respected or rewarded for their efforts. People who engage in these practices are not simply unrewarded but instead are often misunderstood, exploited, or suffer negative career consequences for engaging in these activities. Those who enable others are likely to be characterized by coworkers as "helpful," or "nice" people rather than as competent workers who are contributing to organizational learning. While being viewed as a nice person is hardly grounds for complaint, it has little career capital. "Nice," "helpful," and "thoughtful" are not found on many lists of leadership characteristics. The skill in explaining complicated ideas so that others will be able to understand them is trivialized when labeled as merely "helpful." A holistic view that time spent in enabling another is time well spent is noted not as a competency or an "ideal" way of working but rather as evidence that the worker simply "likes" to do this sort of thing. Skills such as these are dismissed as personal attributes rather than counted as competencies.

It is not only the relational practice of enabling others that gets disappeared in this way. Engineers in the study who, for example, wrote thank you notes to other groups who were providing important resources to the project, were seen as thoughtful or caring people, concerned about others' feelings. Maintaining relationships in this way was not recognized as a value-added activity that potentially prevented future problems and project delays. Others, who spoke of avoiding conflict in order to create an environment where people would feel free to express their ideas, were often characterized not as collaborative team players but as people with dependency issues who were afraid of confrontation because they had a "need to be liked." These examples suggest that rewarding relational skills and creating systems that will foster their development is no easy task. Behavior of this type runs so counter to organizational definitions of competence that simply calling for a new kind of worker is unlikely to lead to change.

This book is not the first to call attention to the difficulty of advocating change that runs counter to deeply held assumptions and beliefs about success. Many others have noted that strong resistance is encountered when underlying assumptions, or what Peter Senge calls "mental models," are challenged.[3] Recently, David Bradford and Allan Cohen, in reflecting on why organizations have not achieved more success in moving toward new models of organizing, note, "Worker empowerment and participative management programs should have recast the system of leadership and followership, but they have not. They have gotten people to think and experiment, but have not achieved significant reform. Outmoded assumptions about the roles of the leader and the followers block transformation."[4]

What these and other prescriptive books on organizational change[5] ignore, and what relational practice and the disappearing dynamic help us to see, is that outmoded assumptions are not the only problem. It is the gendered nature of these assumptions that complicate the problem in invisible but powerful ways. The disappearing dynamic helps us see that there are powerful, gender-linked forces that silence and suppress relational challenges to organizational norms. The result is that behaviors such as relational practice are not merely difficult to encourage in organizations, they are systematically disappeared through a process in which they are coded as private-sphere (feminine) activities that stand outside the public-sphere (masculine) definition of work and competence.

What this means for organizations that are calling for team-oriented, less hierarchical, empowered workers is that they are unlikely to get them from current practice, regardless of calls for transformation. Failure to recognize the new behavior as evidence of competence, the lack of language to describe it as such, and the coding of such behavior as feminine, are powerful dynamics undermining efforts to restructure work and the workplace in this way. Transformation, then, will require far more than an exhortation to change organizational culture or re-engineer the work process. It will require an acknowledgment of and an engagement with the complex, gendered forces underlying current organizational norms. Without such an acknowledgment, efforts to disrupt these structures are likely to fail.

Why? Because the changes needed are neither benign nor gender-neutral. They are radical in a way that is not often recognized by the popular management books, even those that acknowledge the feminine nature of the new requirements, such as Sally Helgesen's book on the female advantage and Judy Rosener's on women's competitive advantage.[6] The disappearing dynamic highlights that the ways organizations would have to adapt to foster new ways of working are radical—not only because these ideas challenge some of our deepest assumptions about work but also because they challenge some of our deepest assumptions about ourselves as good men and women. They engage what Virginia Valian calls gender schemas, "intuitive hypotheses about the behaviors, traits, and preferences of men and women,"[7] and gender roles or the expectations we have about the way these sets of behaviors interact, support, and complement each other. They engage powerful beliefs about the separation of work and personal life and what kind of personal characteristics it takes to succeed in each of these spheres.[8] These are the forces that disappear relational practice. Getting beyond disappearing, then, requires a strategy for change that encompasses these different dimensions of gender and moves beyond the gender-neutral language often used to define the issues and prescribe solutions. In other words, it requires addressing the gender implications and differential impact of the disappearing dynamic on men and women in the new organization.

Discussing the gender implications of moving beyond disappearing, however, requires a cautionary note. It is important to recall that relational practice is not about sex differences. It would be unwise as well as unwarranted to draw essentialist, biologically based conclusions about men and women based on the findings from this fieldwork. The study includes no data on how men experience these phenomena, on the extent to which women—as opposed to men—enact relational practice, or the extent to which the notion of relational practice influences male experience. The findings, in other words, need to be understood not as a story about the intentions or characteristics of men versus women, but rather, as an example of how the masculine logic underlying organizational practices shapes the experience and understanding of what is seen as important work in organizations, with potentially negative consequences for women, men, and the organization. Thus, the story the findings tell is how phenomena that fail to fit the masculine ideal get disappeared and devalued in organizational settings.

Of course there is one important way in which women do not fit this masculine ideal. While there may be, and undoubtedly are, many men who do not fit it behaviorally, all women fail to fit it physically. In fact, it was for precisely this reason—the way in which women were operating at the "line of fault" between "women" and "worker"—that women were chosen as subjects for the study. Within this context, and even in the absence of data about men, it is important to discuss the gender implications of the findings for women and for organizations.

The most obvious gender implication is in the disappearing dynamic itself. While both men and women might believe in the value of relational practice and have the skills to enact it, only women, by virtue of their subject position as women, are expected to work this way. In other words, the disappearing dynamic has especially powerful consequences for women. Indeed, the twists and turns of this dynamic help us see the inner workings of the glass ceiling quite vividly. When women enact relational practice, a vicious cycle begins. They enact relational practice, but instead of being seen as competent workers, their behavior is misunderstood and conflated with femininity. Women experience two negative effects from this association with the feminine. One, they fear the label "feminine" because femininity is routinely considered inappropriate to the workplace. Second, they fear being exploited by the expectation that they will operate out of a context of mutuality where none exists. If they try another strategy, acting in a way that is more traditionally masculine and fits better with organizational norms, they experience something different but equally negative. They are likely to be labeled arrogant, bitchy, or brash—common attributions for stepping out of the bounds of femininity. They are caught in a bind, or what Ann Morrison and her associates at the Center for Creative Leadership call *the narrow band.*[9]

However, the disappearing of relational practice helps us see that the dilemma women face in the workplace is more complicated than the narrow band. It is not only that women have to find ways of working that label them both feminine and fit for the job or that they have been socialized to operate in a different sphere of life and have developed relational skills. As strong as these two forces are, the study suggests that there is another reason women work or seek to work in ways that differ from organizational norms: their belief in an alternative model of effectiveness. In other words, the findings indicate *three* forces underlying women's motivation to enact relational practice:

- *Expectations:* The expectation they will act relationally;
- *Skills:* The skill set to do so;
- *Beliefs:* A belief in a relational model of effectiveness.

It is the interplay among these three forces that has special implications for women who would like to strategize ways out of the dilemmas they face in the workplace. While the narrow band suggests some strategies that might address the first two—the way in which women are expected to act relationally and because of socialization practices have the skills to do so effectively—it ignores the third and perhaps most powerful force underlying relational practice: the belief system in which connection is viewed as a primary route to effectiveness. It is the addition of this third force—the model of growth, achievement, and effectiveness motivating the behavior—that makes the discussion of the disappearing dynamic and its implications for organizations so significant. It is the belief system, and the different model of success it offers, that gives form to the real challenge in relational practice and helps to envision different structures, practices, and work processes. The belief system is the real casualty in the disappearing dynamic, disappearing this challenge to organizational norms. Strategies to resist the disappearing dynamic must take account of this third force and move beyond narrow-band responses to gender dynamics in the workplace.

Moving beyond narrow-band strategies for success is a challenge. It is one thing to develop strategies that will help women resist being dismissed as too feminine to survive or to be effective in the workplace. Certainly, traditional self-help manuals written for women managers are replete with suggestions of this type. Strategies that help them resist the masculine nature of organizational norms—without getting disappeared—are quite another matter.

The need for new strategies is critical. A number of recent studies indicate that women are increasingly dissatisfied with organizational norms about routes to success and effectiveness and their inability to challenge or change these norms.[10] Whether lawyers, entrepreneurs, or corporate executives, women who have made it to the top playing by the rules are beginning to question the rules themselves. Often, seeing no way out and feeling frustrated by their inability to challenge these norms, they opt to leave. Some leave the paid workforce completely. Others retreat from high-level positions to take jobs lower in the hierarchy, such as returning to teaching after spending years in educational administration. Others leave to create their own work environments, starting small businesses or working as freelance consultants. Contrary to popular belief, these women do not point to work and family conflict as the main reason for leaving. When interviewed, they talk about their inability to work the way they want to work in the current structure and about the inefficiency and ineffectiveness of many work norms. In other words, it appears that many women, not just the engineers in this study, have a different route to effectiveness they would like to enact in the workplace but feel stymied in their attempts to do so. Looking at this from the perspective of the disappearing dynamic, it is easy to see why.

What strategies are available to women who are caught in the negative effects of the disappearing dynamic? Is there a way to move beyond the choice of either fitting in or moving out? Debra Meyerson and Maureen Scully offer "tempered radicalism" as a way out of the dilemma. Being a tempered radical means challenging the status quo strongly enough to have an impact on it but not so strongly that one cannot succeed within it.[11] They suggest that this type of behavior can be transformational because it is a way of changing organizations from the bottom up, through a process they call everyday leadership. Everyday leaders with radical ideas can challenge norms and create a new organizational reality by using a strategy Karl Weick calls "small wins."[12] In terms of relational practice, this strategy means pushing on organizational norms in a way that would challenge these norms but would take into account the practical realities of being a woman in a predominantly masculine value system.

When I give presentations on relational practice to groups of women, the discussions of these practical realities become quite lively. Women have many stories to tell about the dilemmas of working in masculine environments and are eager to brainstorm strategies for change. In the course of these discussions, it is apparent that many have become quite adept at challenging masculine norms in small but persistent ways, without getting disappeared, exploited, or dismissed. They are happy to hear they are not alone and are eager to help each other work out dilemmas. These spontaneous brainstorming sessions are a nice reminder of the power of gathering together to talk about these issues with others. As someone comfortable in more theoretical domains, I have learned much in these discussions about the practical realities of pushing back on the disappearing dynamic. Although these stories of "practical pushing" were not part of the original data, I have gathered them here and grouped them loosely into four strategies: naming, norming, negotiating, and networking. I have generalized these stories and describe them as principles, with a recognition that this is an extremely preliminary typology. We need more stories. Where appropriate, I have disguised the examples to protect the anonymity of the women and their organizations. These examples are offered as a way of learning from each others' "small wins" so that we, together, can continue to tell the story of relational practice.

Practical Pushing: Four Strategies for Success

Naming

Naming is a strategy of calling attention to relational practice as work, i.e., intentional action to increase effectiveness. There are three naming strategies that cover the what, how and who of relational practice.

Name Relational Practice Using a Language of Competence   Name the behavior using language that reflects competence. Developing a language of competence to capture the complexity and skill involved in working from a model of growth-in-connection is a good first step in combating the disappearing dynamic. Since many of the behaviors are likely to be misunderstood as personality characteristics rather than competencies, it is important to use language that captures the skill dimensions of this behavior. For example, on hearing these findings one of the engineers in the study decided to make one of the roles she played for her team more visible by talking about it differently. Rather than simply working behind the scenes to make sure key people outside the team were doing their jobs and not feeling exploited, she started to talk of her role as "interfacing." At team meetings she reported regularly on the status of these interfacing efforts, and eventually the practice became so routine that others adopted the term, and it was put on the agenda. In this way she rescued the activity from obscurity and put it on the organizational screen. Other examples of creating new language might include talking of "continuous teaching" as part of organizational learning and noting when you observe others practicing this behavior skillfully. Developing a language of competence is a powerful way of bringing relational skills and behaviors into the organizational domain where they can be recognized and rewarded as evidence of competence.

Name the Intended Outcomes of Relational Practice   Another naming strategy is to call attention to the intended outcomes of relational practice and its "value-added" potential. At a gathering to talk about relational practice, one woman gave a good example of how this strategy could be used. As a team leader, she had given a presentation to top management, intentionally using the pronoun "we" to represent what had in fact been a team effort. She was taken aside afterwards by her mentor and told that she would never get ahead if she didn't "stop with this 'we' stuff." She was told that the presentation would have been a lot stronger if she had used the pronoun "I" because "we" sounds weak and overly general. She was urged to speak more strongly, to not be afraid of "claiming her space" or taking credit for what she had done. As she reflected on this advice, she realized it presented a dilemma. She certainly did not want to disappear the work she had done as team leader in getting the results. Yet she felt the value she added in her team leader role was tied to the way she created an environment where diverse talents and perspectives could be brought to bear on the problem. The result was a genuine team effort, and she felt uncomfortable disappearing that aspect of the work in order to "claim her space." In the discussion, another woman came up with a good strategy for "practical pushing": she used the pronoun "we," but prefaced the presentation with an announcement that she was using this pronoun intentionally to indicate something unique. She was using it to indicate that her recommendations were the result of a productive collective effort and that she was proud of her team for the way they had used all the talent in the group.

What is especially effective about this strategy is that it accomplishes two goals. It makes visible the current organizational norm—which in this case is to use the pronoun "I" to represent team effort—thereby calling attention to a form of self-promotion that is probably taken for granted and rarely noted. Second, it offers an alternative demonstration of competence—competence as a team leader who can foster collective achievement—and also communicates an unwillingness to disappear the contribution of team members. In other words, it calls attention to an alternative but does not leave to chance how the alternative will be interpreted. It makes visible the intent and defines it as an outcome important to the organization. In this instance, it allows the team leader to call attention to the value she added by being a relational practitioner in the way she led the team, without promoting herself at the expense of her team.

Name Relational Practice Others Do   Naming relational practice can extend beyond the self. In fact, calling attention to the disappearing dynamic by naming the skill and intended outcomes of relational practice may be easier—and less risky—when the focus is on others. This strategy can be a powerful way of focusing organizational attention on invisible work and pushing organizational practices beyond current norms. It can also be a way of empowering others and creating allies. There may be many people who are working from a relational model of effectiveness but are unaware of how this behavior gets disappeared. Naming it can create allies who may join in the efforts to challenge masculine practices and norms.

This strategy can be as simple as substituting the word "effective" when someone else notes the "nice" or "sensitive" attributes of a relational practitioner. Or it can mean suggesting more formal ways to document or make visible the invisible contributions others have made. An engineering professor told the story of how she used this strategy when she served on a tenure and promotion committee evaluating the credentials of a fellow faculty member. The candidate being discussed had not calculated the mentoring of female engineering students in her teaching load because the formula did not include this activity. However, letters of appreciation from students—even those not in her classes—indicated that this mentoring made a significant contribution to the department. The committee member pointed out that recruitment and retention of female students was not only a departmental goal but was part of the strategic plan of the college. She noted that mentoring students from other classes, who might not otherwise have a female role model, was an especially important, but invisible contribution to these goals. She suggested a formula that could be used to reflect the added workload. Although the committee rejected the suggestion and refused to recalibrate the candidate's teaching load, the suggestion called attention to the beneficial actions of the candidate. The chair of the committee agreed to include this point in the committee write-up and final evaluation of the candidate.

Naming can feel like a slow and frustrating process. Using the pronoun "we" instead of "I" may have little immediate effect. The unwillingness of the committee to recalculate a professor's teaching load can feel like failure. Practical pushing, however, is a strategy of "small wins," little steps in changing deeply rooted practices that are seen as so normal they are rarely questioned or even noticed. Calling attention to the differential impact of the workload formula—how this particular female engineering faculty is carrying a disproportionate load in helping the unit achieve its stated goal—is only one step in a larger process. It is practical for exactly this reason. By naming what she sees, the committee member creates a small chink in the organizational discourse, opening a space for future action. Perhaps the candidate will be encouraged by the committee write-up and will adopt a language of skill and competence to talk about her work and the value it adds. Perhaps she will sit on future promotion committees where she will advance these ideas. Perhaps another committee member will remember the suggested changes to the formula and become an advocate for these or similar changes in evaluative criteria. Opening space in the organizational discourse to talk about and envision new practices, structures, and norms is an ongoing process. Naming is one important strategy, but it is only the beginning.

Norming

Norming strategies call attention to organizational norms of effectiveness, pointing out the potential costs or unintended negative consequences of these norms and offering different, relationally based alternatives.

Question Organizational Concepts   The first norming strategy is to question fundamental organizational concepts from a relational perspective. Many of these concepts, such as leadership, decision making, and organizational learning, although implicitly relational in nature, are defined in one-sided, nonmutual terms. The customary focus in these relational interactions is on the party with more institutional power. For example, leadership is often defined from the perspective of the leader's impact on others, ignoring concepts such as fluid expertise, mutual empathy, or mutual empowerment. Envisioning leadership from a relational perspective could surface alternative models that incorporate fluid expertise or other relational concepts.

Questioning assumptions from a relational perspective is a good way to call attention to the individualistic, often hierarchical "logic of effectiveness" underlying many organizational practices. Suggesting rotating models of leadership or decision making schema that are based on knowledge rather than positional power or organizational learning models that value "continuous teaching" as well as "continuous learning" are ways to question organizational norms from a relational perspective. Asking "Why not?" when met with incredulous stares from coworkers opens up a discussion of the possible benefits of more relational approaches, as well as the possible negative consequences of current practice. In general, this strategy entails calling attention to the nonrelational norms influencing behavior, suggesting ways these norms might be counterproductive and offering a relational alternative.

A financial analyst shared how she used this strategy to question her department's way of generating options and making decisions. During a meeting to discuss proposals for a new reporting system, a colleague started to point out the flaws in the system she proposed. She objected and asked that she be given a chance to describe the entire proposal before having to defend each point. He smiled and responded in a friendly tone that he was simply trying to be helpful by playing devil's advocate. At first, she accepted this description of his behavior. Playing devil's advocate was a legitimate role and a strong departmental norm. She continued but felt increasingly unable to communicate her ideas effectively. Realizing that the proposal was about to go down in flames without a fair hearing, she stopped mid-sentence and motioned for a time out. She pointed out that this assumption about "truth through conflict" might be counterproductive, and she questioned the legitimacy of playing devil's advocate as the best way to discuss new ideas. She suggested that perhaps they should try being "angel's advocates" for each other when ideas were in the developmental stage, helping to draw out the positive implications of the suggestion and what elements they might want to preserve in the final product. She reported that her comments and the humorous tone in which she made them changed the tenor of the group discussion.

Reflect from a Relational Perspective   Another norming strategy is to reflect on one's own behavior. Questioning "natural" responses to situations can be a good way to understand organizational norms and envision alternative, more relationally based strategies for success. When faced with a problem, reflecting on it from a growth-in-connection perspective can surface options or highlight a formerly invisible course of action. A female vice president of engineering, the only woman at this level in the firm, offers a nice example of this strategy. In her first week on the job she was asked to make a "ship product" decision for her group. She was in a quandary. She knew she had not yet proven herself to the group, which had few females in it and had never had a female manager. She understood that group members would be using the occasion to evaluate her leadership potential. She had all the information in terms of reports and raw data that was needed to make the decision. However, being new to the job, she also knew she was lacking a number of important contextual factors. She felt pressure to be decisive to demonstrate her leadership ability and her willingness to "make the tough decisions"—traits she knew were important in the organization. On the other hand, she did not feel confident making the decision based on the data she had.

Reflecting on her dilemma from a relational perspective helped her see that the norm about leaders not admitting to a need for help was holding her back from doing what she thought was best for the project. After some thought she devised a practical pushing strategy. She called a meeting of her staff and used a language of competence to "name" her relational solution. She said she wanted to acknowledge the "local knowledge" that resided in the group and the expertise each of them had, especially expertise that might not be reflected in the hard data. She asked each in turn to look at the data from their unique perspective and give a "ship/no ship" recommendation. She assured them that she would make the decision and take the heat if it turned out to be wrong. However, she wanted to create a working environment where people could bring all their knowledge—tacit as well as hard data—to the table. She asked them to give their honest opinion of the situation. In looking back on this strategy, she feels it worked well. She is proud that she resisted the temptation to demonstrate competence in a way that might have had negative consequences for the project. She demonstrated a new norm for the group—being an expert means admitting what you don't know and creating a team environment where you can get the facts from those who do.

As this example illustrates, making a conscious effort to develop relational skills and a repertoire of relational work practices may mean adopting a different, more mutual stance toward others. However, approaching work relationships from a standpoint of mutuality and implicit reciprocity rather than one of autonomy and competition can be risky. Being conscious of the disappearing dynamic and using practical pushing strategies such as "naming" and "norming" can diminish some of the personal risk. Nonetheless, it is important to remember the political implications of relational behavior within current organizational power structures. When done intentionally and with an awareness of organizational power dynamics, there are a number of ways to try new things and develop relational skills without hurting your career.

One opportunity to enhance relational skills is to actively seek out chances to contribute to the growth, well-being, or achievement of another. This goal could be accomplished in a formal way by offering to share information or knowledge with a coworker. It could also be accomplished more informally by interacting with others in ways that communicate a willingness to learn from them. Stepping out of the "expert" role to signal an openness to being influenced by others can build relational capital in unexpected ways. A new executive director describes how being open to learning from her associate director not only helped her succeed in her new position, it was perceived as mentoring by the associate. The director, having a more traditional view of mentoring, was surprised to discover that simply allowing the associate to see how much she was learning from her and giving her credit for what she contributed was experienced by the associate as mentoring. As one of the few senior women in her organization she had often felt guilty for not taking a more active role in mentoring younger women. It had always seemed like a time-consuming role, one that her family responsibilities did not allow. Practicing "fluid expertise" however, was a different story. This type of mutual empowering felt natural, not time consuming. It was a way of working with people that felt authentic and sensible. She reports that thinking of mentoring in this way has changed her view of herself and of others. She now sees mentoring as a by-product of working effectively. She makes an effort to enact this kind of mutuality and fluid expertise whenever she can and to respond to it and name it when she experiences it in others.[13]

Another approach to developing relational skills is to seek out opportunities to integrate rather than dichotomize the public and private spheres in our own lives by modifying and using at work the skills we have learned in our private lives. This could include focusing on feelings as a source of data and then using these data to strategize a more effective response to a situation or practicing empathic listening to understand another's emotional context or anticipate what others might feel in response a situation. Additional strategies to hone relational skills, while at the same time enhancing effectiveness, might include consciously making an effort to build on rather than compete with others' ideas or suggestions, or consciously responding to others in ways that honestly and authentically affirm their contribution. An even more challenging developmental task would be to make a concerted effort to not disappear the help—including the embedded outcomes—that others have contributed to our achievements.

Maureen Harvey, a colleague who has been building her own relational skills in organizations for years notes that it is important to remember that relational practice is a technique of authenticity. She cautions that there is a temptation when trying to build these skills to lose the authenticity that is an essential part of relational interaction and perhaps fall back on dysfunctional patterns of relationality, often confusing being relational with being nice or selfless. She says she continually needs to remind herself that the goal is an empowered self-in-connection, not selflessness. She gives examples of what she means by an authentic, empowered self when she reminds herself and others to use "we" when referring to group achievement only when it *is* group achievement, to ask for help only when we *want* help and to "not disappear" others' contributions to our efforts only when there *are* contributions.[14]

Practicing this new behavior is particularly challenging for women because it requires us to create new models of work relationships based on principles of authenticity and mutuality, principles that have not been part of gender socialized behavior in patriarchal systems.[15] In other words, it requires that we adopt principles that are themselves evolving and being redefined through efforts to enact relational practice in workplace settings.

Negotiating

Another way of resisting the disappearing dynamic is to negotiate around it. A partner in an accounting firm describes how she used this strategy. She notes that in her firm women are often asked to take on ad hoc assignments that entail relational work. These tasks usually have a human resource function, such as heading a selection or search committee, overseeing an employee-appreciation initiative, coordinating a United Way campaign, or being the outplacement liaison during a reorganization. Because women have the relational skills to do these jobs well and because they recognize the value of doing them well, they often accept. Only later do they discover that although these assignments have been described in developmental terms, they have little career capital. Others who have done more traditional developmental tasks are viewed as having added more value to bottom-line goals and objectives. She describes this as a complicated double bind. While she wants to say yes to such requests, she knows it is not in her best interest to do so. It is complicated by the fact that in her firm one of the ways to demonstrate commitment and loyalty is to "never say no" when asked to take on special assignments. This apparently gender-neutral cultural norm indeed has a gender bias. She notes that her male partners may experience negative career consequences if they refuse special assignments. Female partners, because of the relational nature of the assignments offered, experience negative career consequences whether they say no *or* yes.

The practical pushing strategy she found and now advises other women to adopt is to negotiate a way out of the dilemma. This is the strategy she used when she was asked to take on a special year-long human resource initiative. The opportunity was described as developmental, giving her national visibility and a chance to interact with top management. Saying no meant she would go on record as having passed up a developmental opportunity. But in an environment where "rainmaking"—or generating client revenue—is the most important measure of success, saying yes meant she was likely to be invisible in the next round of promotions. She believed the job was important and that she could do it well. She decided to negotiate conditions that would allow her to say yes without getting disappeared. In responding to the request she expressed her appreciation at having been given the opportunity to take on such valuable work. She enumerated the relational competencies necessary to do the job well and expressed pleasure in being recognized for having these skills. However, she added, it was common knowledge that, although she and her boss knew otherwise, these types of assignments were often regarded as less valuable to the bottom line and she worried about the career implication. She proposed a plan for calculating the costs and benefits of the initiative and a formula, using her last year's revenue as a base, to generate a "rain-making equivalency," to be used in assessing her contribution. When her boss expressed surprise at the hard line she was taking because he assumed she would want to do this job, she assured him that indeed she did want the job. She just wanted to make sure was recognized for the value it would add.

Deborah Kolb,[16] an expert in gender and negotiation describes this negotiation strategy as "always say yes." The strategy is to identify the conditions of an enthusiastic "yes," leaving it up to the other party to meet the conditions, negotiate a compromise, or withdraw the offer. It is particularly effective as a practical pushing strategy because it makes several different aspects of the disappearing dynamic visible. It creates an opportunity to

• name relational skills using a language of competency,
• make visible the norm of "not saying no" and the differential impact of this norm on women and men, and
• push back on the disappearing of relational work by assigning a monetary value to relational competence.

Networking

Networking, the fourth practical pushing strategy, requires forming growth-in-connection networks of support to encourage and foster relational practice. Relational practitioners who have been made to feel inadequate, naïve or ashamed for their efforts to work in a context of mutuality, often find it difficult to "know what they know." Trusting their instincts, when the organizational system is giving them error messages for doing so, is tough. A number of relational practitioners have found that forming a support group inside or outside the immediate work environment is helpful and empowering. The director of a university-sponsored research institute formed such a group. She gathers a small number of female senior administrators from area colleges and universities to meet monthly. They each bring a dilemma or leadership issue to discuss. The group considers each dilemma and brainstorms practical pushing strategies, taking the gender dimensions of the disappearing dynamic into account. She reports that this format is practical as well as supportive. Using it, they have been able to help each other identify relational behavior and create a language of competence to talk about it. It has also helped them to identify the assumptions behind some of their dilemmas and brainstorm ways to challenge nonrelational norms without getting disappeared. Members appreciate the solution-oriented focus of the group and contrast it with other support groups that, without a growth-fostering orientation such as relational practice, have been less energizing and empowering.

There is an advantage in establishing a relational practitioners' support group outside the immediate work environment. An outside group, as opposed to one within the organization, can allay some of the concerns women have about belonging to such groups. Women, especially those who have made it to upper levels in the organization, often shun groups that could be stigmatized as "women's groups" or have been identified with women's issues. Unfortunately, there is good reason for their reluctance. These groups are often viewed negatively within organizations. This presents a dilemma because there are also real advantages to meeting with people internal to the organization: Group strategies can be devised around similar issues, a common language can begin to take hold, and the same organizational concepts and assumptions can be questioned from a number of different sources. In other words, an internal group has greater potential to be a force for change within an organization and can make a real difference in how things are done and work is perceived. For this reason, many have found ways of working around the problem of being stigmatized as a "women's group." Some have invited male colleagues to join, while others have met off site, either for a monthly lunch or late afternoon tea. Another innovative solution is to establish an on-line chat room with members both internal and external to the organization.

The important point is that wherever and however it is created, a system of support is essential to sustain a strategy of practical pushing, especially for women. A colleague points out that in her experience the men she works with who try relational practice have more latitude in getting their behavior viewed as competence. Not only are they granted more freedom in terms of trying something different, taking risks, and making mistakes, they can also retreat back to masculine patterns of interaction and control without being labeled bitchy or arrogant. Operating under different constraints, she finds she as a woman needs a network of support to which she can retreat, a network of colleagues who will help her identify the systemic issues she is experiencing and devise practical ways of pushing back on problematic masculine norms rather than simply adapting to them.

Organizational Strategies for Success

For organizations that have recognized the need for relational practice, a number of systemic interventions can be adopted. These steps require the support of upper management and entail symbolic as well as structural leverage points. The goal is to change the organizational culture in a way that would encourage relational practice, not only among those who might be inclined toward this way of working but also, and perhaps more importantly, among those not so inclined.

Demonstrate the Value of Relational Practice from the Top Down   Given the complicated dynamic in which relational practice gets coded as feminine and inappropriate to the workplace, encouraging this behavior is not something that can be accomplished by directive. Rhetoric alone is not sufficient. To combat the strong, gendered forces aligned against it, women and men must feel assured that demonstrating relational competence is something that will enhance rather than diminish their career prospects.

One way to align relational behavior with positive career outcomes is to showcase it—or the need and benefits of it—in top management. There are many mainstream efforts to do this. One-on-one executive development programs, such as those suggested by Robert Kaplan[17] and Joan

Kofodimus[18] encourage self-reflection by exploring the parallels between behavior patterns in one's work life and those exhibited in one's private life. Books such as Dan Goleman's *Emotional Intelligence* and Steven Covey's *Seven Habits of Highly Successful People* highlight the need for relational skills and the costs to organizations of not having them.[19] Programs that promote these ideas and offer workshops to help people identify and develop relational skills are an important step in taking relational practice seriously. However, the limitations of these mainstream efforts in counteracting the disappearing dynamic are similar to the limitations of "female advantage" efforts. Describing the value of relational practice is one thing, recognizing the gender/power dynamics inherent in it is quite another. Adding a gender dimension to these self-development programs is essential if they are to achieve real results. Without an awareness of the role gender identity plays in the disappearing dynamic, even so-called enlightened management practice may reinforce gender roles and the differential impact of the dynamic on women. Relational practice is not gender-neutral behavior. It is behavior that engages deeply held gender identities and beliefs. A relational practice developmental program for senior executives, to be truly effective, needs to include reflective exercises on the way society in general and their organizations in particular often use women's relational skills as a free resource.[20] Jennifer Pierce gives a compelling account of this gender dynamic in her description of how female paralegals are expected to perform their jobs. She notes that male paralegals are not expected to mother or nurture the lawyers they support. Women, on the other hand, are routinely required to exhibit mothering behavior and offer feminine versions of support such as reassuring, anticipating needs, or responding to feelings. Although required to perform this work and criticized when their behavior does not meet gendered norms, they are not rewarded or recognized for this extra work.[21]

Adding gender-related vignettes such as this to self-development programs for top management can foster an understanding of the disappearing dynamic as a systemic rather than an individual issue. One CEO, in doing such an exercise saw that the way his organization clustered women in support roles was rooted in a more general phenomenon: people's personal histories and early life experience of supportive environments. He was asked to reflect on why the entire secretarial force in his operation was female. He responded that from his personal perspective he would not want a male secretary. He would prefer a woman, he said, because he wanted someone who would get some satisfaction and self-esteem from helping him do a good job. A male, he felt, would be more likely to be worried about accomplishing his own tasks and would be less willing to do "whatever it took" to support him. This recognition of the important role support plays in achievement, and the value it adds to an organization was an important turning point in this personal development program. Reflecting on what it would mean if all members of an organization, at all levels in the hierarchy, received satisfaction and self-esteem from empowering others to achieve changed his view of the central problem and gave him a new vision of a relationally proficient organization. At the same time, he recognized how his feelings of comfort with female support staff were based in gender expectations formed early in life. This helped him appreciate the deeply rooted nature of this gender dynamic.

The recognition that the organization reinforced the dynamic by clustering expectations of support in women helped him see how women, even at higher levels in the organization, might be expected to support others with no prospect of reciprocal encouragement. In brainstorming leverage points for change, he thought of ideas such as demonstrating through his own behavior that he was willing to support someone else in a "crunch time" by, for example, doing some routine calculations or even offering to get lunch or coffee for analysts who were preparing client reports. He also considered more systemic interventions, such as including a category of support activities on the performance appraisal forms requiring "examples of how you have helped coworkers achieve organizational goals." Perhaps most important, he saw that developmental assignments to help people acquire relational skills can be a real benefit to the organization. Rather than offer female staff opportunities to use their relational skills in human resource functions, for example, it might be better to offer these opportunities to male "fast trackers."

Recognize the Present Value Relational Activity Adds to Organizational Effectiveness   A number of recent studies make visible the hidden relational work that is done in organizations.[22] Each of these studies emphasizes that the current paradigm of organizations-as-instrumental-entities is an incomplete representation of organizational life. Each identifies different ways in which organizations depend on and reap the benefits of relational activity. However, the fact that these activities are systematically devalued and their effect on the efficiency and effectiveness of organizational action remains invisible and unrewarded inhibits organizations from taking positive actions to promote more of this activity in its members. Yet, with a workforce that has been trained to overvalue hierarchy, individualism, and competition, this is exactly what is needed.

One high-tech company recently undertook such an initiative. Working with members of the Stone Center for Developmental Services and Studies at Wellesley College, a group of software engineers participated in a program to bring relational strengths into mainstream organizational values and structures. The project drew on employee experience, particularly the experience of women, to identify relational activities that were unrecognized and unrewarded in the current structure. The resulting eighteen recommendations for change, ranging from rewarding teamwork to the establishment of support groups, made an appreciable difference in the culture of the participating work group. Project members speak of a sense of empowerment and an ability to bring "more of themselves" to work. Organizations that undertake such initiatives, in which the present value of relational activity is recognized, can make significant progress in legitimizing and thereby encouraging the type of growth-in-connection that is central to relational practice.[23]

Address the Issue of Work and Personal Life Integration   Although growth-in-connection can take place in organizational contexts, recent research suggests that many people experience this type of learning in personal relationships and transfer it to organizational settings. For example, those who have studied the sociology of caring suggest that caring for others encourages a holistic approach to understanding and responding to events, an approach that develops an ability to integrate emotional, cognitive, and behavioral data in forming a response.[24] Interestingly, a recent study of service workers found that those who were able to assume this holistic approach, or what was called "total responsibility" for the work, were those who were involved in some sort of caretaking activity outside of work, such as parenting, coaching, or being a team leader in a youth group.[25] This suggests that organizations intent on developing relational skills in their workers might do so through the systematic encouragement of all individuals to be involved in caretaking work.

Perhaps even more important to organizations, however, are the consequences of inhibiting the development of these skills. Relational proficiency requires practice in mutuality and experience in contributing to the development of others. The increase in self-esteem, the positive energy that comes from mutual connection, and the stretching and growing that occurs for people involved in caring relationships are, as Jean Baker Miller asserts, essential developmental experiences underlying relational proficiency.[26] If inhibited by organizational conditions that (even unintentionally) discourage family- or community-related activities, individuals will be limited in their ability to grow in these ways. On the other hand, organizations whose practices, structures, and policies value the integration of work and personal work are more likely to have employees who bring more fully developed selves to the workplace.

Taking this a step further, one could imagine, for example, that in a work environment where relational skills were on par with technical skills, developmental programs might include some form of family or community involvement as a necessary condition of advancement or continued employment. Performance appraisals could include suggestions for meeting this relational developmental need by the use of "outside consultants" (e.g., children, elderly parents, members of shelters, and staff of schools and hospitals). This radical idea would be self-reinforcing. Those caring for others would develop relational skills. If organizations rewarded those skills and linked them to specific competencies and developmental career plans this might encourage others to strive to acquire these skills through similar means.

Strategies: Summary Implications

Readers may have reacted with skepticism or amusement to the suggestion that organizations relax the work-family boundary in order to develop relational skills in workers. Within an organizational discourse of costs, benefits, and global competition, it is not surprising that these suggestions might be seen as naïve or far-fetched. It is important to pay attention to this reaction because it highlights the most powerful implication of the findings. The suggestion that relaxing the work-family boundary might be in an organization's best interest is startling because it is a challenge to an organizational assumption that is rarely questioned: the necessity of keeping a strict boundary between the public and private spheres of life.[27] These assumptions manifest themselves in organizational norms, structures, and practices that maintain a series of socially constructed separations that implicitly assign one set of tasks and associated behaviors to women and another to men. Challenging these norms, then, challenges not only the separation but also the deeply held, gender-linked assumptions that maintain that separation. It challenges the status quo because it calls attention to how organizations rely on this separation in order to continue using gender as a free resource.

In other words, focusing on our skepticism that it would be in an organization's best interest to encourage work and personal life integration helps us see that taking relational practice seriously will require a major rethinking of organizational norms. These norms manifest themselves in structures and practices that simultaneously encourage the false separation and *inhibit the integration* of gendered dichotomies such as masculine/feminine, public sphere/private sphere, and even support activities/achievement activities. More to the point, these separations reinforce society's contradictory message that relational activity is not needed but women must provide it—a contradiction that implicitly entitles organizations to use female gender as a free resource.

For example, gender-linked expectations of supportive behavior allow organizations to absorb the work generated by these expectations (such as relational practice) without rewarding it or even naming it as competence. Organizations also use gender as a resource by clustering support positions at the bottom of the hierarchy, perpetuating the myth of individual achievement, thereby allowing and even encouraging individuals to disappear help they have been given. Finally, organizations use gender as a resource by relying on gender socialization to assign women the task of producing the next generation of workers and then systematically excluding them from positions of power and influence because of their commitment to family. In a complementary way, organizations use male gender as a free resource when they rely on male gender socialization to reinforce the primacy of paid work as a source of achievement and self-esteem.[28]

Organization Theory: Future Directions

This study of relational practice identifies several potentially promising areas for future organizational research. The first is related to the disappearing of relational practice as work. Although the findings cannot support a claim that relational practice exists or gets disappeared in all organizational settings, they certainly suggest that looking for relational practices—even in settings as unlikely as engineering firms—might expand current understandings of many organizational concepts. Using the tenets of relational theory to study the relational dimensions of these concepts could offer a more sophisticated representation of many workplace interactions. For example, the concept of mutuality that is fundamental to growth-in-connection models of development suggests that the one-directional representation or workplace interactions often found in organizational theory is limiting. It does not allow for a differentiation between growth-fostering and non-growth-fostering interactions or a way of capturing the action, interaction, and involvement of both parties. For example, Victoria Parker used relational theory's conceptualization of mutuality to identify the relational work that patients do in the doctor-patient relationship and the effect this has on the quality of care.[29]

Using relational theory's two-directional model could offer new ways of understanding the outcomes of other relational interactions in the workplace such as those inherent in communities of practice, multi-functional teams, leadership, strategic alliance, or collaborations.[30] In addition, differentiating the many aspects of mutuality such as empathy, authenticity, empowerment, and fluid expertise could be used to begin developing a typology of the attributes of high-quality or growth-fostering relationships as differentiated from low-quality or non-growth-fostering relationships.[31]

The second future direction organizational theorists might explore is related to power and gender equity. The issue of gender equity in organizational theory is most often studied through an analysis of the glass ceiling—that is, an analysis of the factors in organizations that are problematic for the professional progress of women.[32] However, the disappearing of relational practice suggests that the factors inhibiting women's progress in organizations are not only problematic for women: They are problematic for organizational effectiveness as well. The process of devaluing work that is associated with the feminine and reifying work associated with the masculine has probably produced many other routine but ineffective work practices—that is, practices that are in place not because they are particularly effective but because they are in line with masculine norms of behaving. In other words, disappearing acts not only disappear relational practice, they disappear the costs of doing business as usual.

In theoretical terms, this links the issue of gender asymmetry (the way that devaluing the feminine is part of what it means to define oneself as masculine) with organizational effectiveness. Theorists interested in promoting organizational effectiveness, might do well to explore other dimensions of organizational culture that manifest masculine traits. By studying these phenomena and understanding that devalued (feminine) possibilities might be getting disappeared, they may uncover new solutions to organizational problems.

Research further theorizing the link between organizational effectiveness and gender asymmetry could lead not only to new understanding of organizational phenomena but also a new class of interventions aimed at fostering gender equity. Many other approaches to gender equity suggest interventions based on principles of fairness and equality. Equalizing power inequities often translates into giving women the same opportunity as men to ignore or devalue the private side of themselves. Examples of this type of intervention would be child care centers that offer evening and weekend hours so parents can spend endless hours at work, or making assertiveness training workshops available to women who are considered too "soft" on employees. Theorizing and locating the problem of gender equity at the level of gender asymmetry might suggest some different types of interventions, in the spirit of those suggested in the previous section. For example, from this perspective, equalizing power inequities between the sexes would mean abandoning the use of female gender as a free and under-appreciated resource. In concrete terms this might mean something as simple as expecting formal and informal support activities to be recognized and encouraged at all levels and adding this formerly invisible work to performance evaluations. Since gender-related power in this perspective would reside in the masculine nature of definitions of "real" work, reducing power inequity would mean redefining "real" work to include these supportive dimensions, or redefining "outcomes" to include outcomes embedded in other people. Power differences and gender segregation would be further reduced if competence in relational or support work were recognized regardless of the sex of the person who exhibits it, rather than one sex being seen as demonstrating caring, while the other is seen as demonstrating competence.

The final direction for future research suggested by this study of relational practice has to do with its use of a stereotypically feminine model of effectiveness. While it was useful for this study to articulate a model of effectiveness based on stereotypically feminine characteristics associated with activity in the private sphere, the fact that these two spheres are usually studied as separate and distinct domains is problematic. Because of this separation, notions of relationality are derived from stereotypical images of femininity influenced by women's role in the private sphere. By definition this means that relational knowledge has not been adequately informed or influenced by the other sphere. As a result, organizational theorists tend to rely on models of collaborations, nurturing, enabling, and contributing to the development of another that are rooted in idealized images of femininity. I believe this has blinded us to new models and has ignored some potentially interesting dimensions of relational interactions. For example, can we imagine a relational re-presentation of concepts such as competition, conflict, or autonomy that does not place these concepts in opposition to relationality but attempts instead to articulate something new? Research intended to articulate these concepts from a relational perspective (i.e., so they meet relational criteria for growth-in-connection, such as mutuality, fluid expertise, and the achievement of the "five good things") would be an important step in refining the relational model of effectiveness presented here. However, I believe that even these tenets of relational theory do not adequately challenge the idealized notions of affection, caring, and altruism that underlie many images of relational activity. All too often, these idealized images result in relational malpractice in the workplace rather than relational practice. To address this issue, further research is needed to unpack the role of emotion and refine the tenets of relational theory in order to continue the task of differentiating growth-fostering from non-growth-fostering relational interactions.

Notes

Preface

1. Follett 1924.
2. Drucker 1996, p. 1.
3. Kanter 1996, p. xvi.
4. Child 1996, p. 88.

Introduction

1. Jack Welch is quoted in Slater 1994, p. 108.

2. For a description of the many different kinds of intelligence needed for effective practice, see Gardner 1993.

3. See, for example, Goleman 1995 and Sternberg 1985.

4. The transitive use of the verb "to disappear" is used to convey agency and make clear a distinction between being invisible and getting disappeared. Although awkward, I could find no better way to convey the sense that the behavior in question is not simply invisible or behind the scenes. Instead, it is *acted on* by a system of practices, norms, and common understandings that suppress its impact and contribution.

5. The glass ceiling is a term coined by Morrison et al. 1987. They used it in the title of their book to describe the invisible barrior women encounter in moving into the higher echelons of corporate management.

Chapter 1

1. See Bailyn 1977.

2. As an example, think of how common it is to see studies about the causes or ill effects of poverty and how rare it is to read studies about the causes or ill

effects of consumerism. Or how many studies of managerial behavior and effectiveness are conducted from the perspective of the manager rather than those who are managed.

3. Jordan et al. 1991, p. vi.

4. Miller 1976, pp. 23–24.

5. See Kanter 1977.

6. See for example, Calvert and Ramsey 1992; Fierman 1990; Grant 1988; Helgesen 1990; Rosener 1990.

7. See Calás and Smircich 1991.

8. Fletcher 1994.

9. Pierce 1996, p. 71.

10. Miller 1976, pp. 79–80, addresses this issue eloquently in *Toward a New Psychology of Women* when she says,

It may be important to differentiate [relational theory] . . . from other ideas. . . . For example . . . Yin and Yang, Jung's notion of the hidden woman in every man and vice versa . . . [and] the opposition of agency and community. . . . Christopher Lasch has described a period when, in response to the first wave of feminism it was advocated that women move into public affairs to do "social housekeeping" for the society, in order to bring their cleanliness and morality into the corrupt world. These formulations fail to take seriously the inequality of power and authority between men and women. It is hardly women's task to go into the dominant culture to "cleanse" it of its problems. This would merely be repetition in another form of "doing for others" and "cleaning" for others—now cleaning up the "body politic. . . ." The notions of Jung and others deny the basic inequality and asymmetry that exist; they are also ahistorical. . . . The present divisions and separations are, I believe, a product of culture as we have known it—that is, a culture based on a primary inequity. It is the very nature of this dichotomization that is in question.

11. A colleague, Roy Jacques, from the University of Massachusetts, introduced me to this body of work he and his mentors, Linda Smircich and Marta Calás used to critique organization studies. His disdain for the "female advantage" literature and Linda and Marta's critique of this approach forced me to think about the issue in a more sophisticated way, resulting in the article I wrote on castrating the female advantage. Their work was critical to the early formulation of my ideas and has continued to influence my work. For readers interested in provocative reading, guaranteed to push the boundaries of their thinking about gender and management, I recommend Calás and Smircich 1993 and 1996; Jacobsen and Jacques 1997; and Jacques 1996.

12. See Lukes 1974, p. 24.

13. See Mumby and Putnam 1992.

14. See Martin and Knopoff 1995.

15. The fieldwork was funded by the Ford Foundation through research grant #910-1036.

Chapter 2

1. Discourse refers to the social arena in which common understandings are manifest in language, social practices, and structures.

2. Ewick and Silbey 1995.

3. Fairclough 1989, p. 17, describes discursive practice as "language as social practice determined by social structures."

4. See Clegg 1989, p. 151.

5. This description of poststructuralist inquiry is necessarily abbreviated. For readers interested in a more comprehensive—but still readable—overview of this perspective, I recommend Alvesson and Deetz 1996 and Flax 1990. For a more thorough discussion of the issues of power and resistance, see Clegg 1989; Collinson 1994; Foucault 1980. For a more detailed explanation of the relationship between ideology, culture and language and ways of destabilizing this relationship, see Ewick and Silbey 1995; Fairclough 1989; Jacobsen and Jacques 1997; Mumby 1988. For a review of the contradictions and dilemmas in using poststructuralist precepts to further feminist study, see Diamond and Quinby 1988 and Weedon 1987.

6. Taylor 1911; Weber 1964.

7. The exemplar of this type of model can be found in Vroom-Yetten 1973.

8. The foundational work on the use of time span as a measure of value is in the typology offered by Eliot Jaques 1979.

9. Morgan 1983.

10. See, for example, Ferguson 1984; Jacobsen and Jacques 1989; Mills and Tancred 1992; Smircich 1985.

11. See March and Olsen 1976.

12. See March and Simon 1958.

13. See Harding 1986 for a discussion of the public and private dichotomy. For a more nuanced analysis of the role gender plays in constructing images of exemplary workers, see Acker 1990.

14. See Parsons and Bales 1955 for the foundational work on this view of the separate spheres as complementary. For a more recent analysis, see Bellah et al. 1985 or Perrow 1986.

15. See, for example, Bradley 1989; Ferguson 1984; Game and Pringle 1983; Harding 1987; Hartmann 1983; Weedon 1987.

16. For a full discussion of the social construction of gender, see Lorber 1991.

17. See, for example, Daniels 1987; DeVault 1990; Game and Pringle 1983; Wadel 1979.

18. See, for example, Bailyn 1993; Bailyn et al. 1996 and 1997; Bradley 1993; Fletcher and Bailyn 1996; Friedlander 1994; Parkin 1993.

19. Many who have studied the structural dimensions of caring, such as Marjorie DeVault's (1990) study of the work involved in feeding the family, Sara Ruddick's (1989) work on maternal thinking and the nursing literature on caring (Benner et al. 1996; Benner and Wrubel 1989; Reverby 1987; Roberts 1990), note that the assumption of affect makes invisible many of the complex, cognitive aspects of the work itself. By the same token, Steven Fineman (1993) and Dennis Mumby and Linda Putnam (1992) note that models of organizational phenomena are constructed as if human emotion were not an influence.

20. For the foundational work on how patriarchy manifests itself in organizational bureaucracy, see Ferguson 1984. For more detail on the gendered nature of the split between the public and private spheres and its relationship to patriarchy, see Acker 1989; Bradley 1989, 1993; Cockburn 1991; Collinson and Hearn 1994; Connell 1995; Gherardi 1995; Lorber 1991; Martin 1995, 1996; Parkin 1993.

21. Chodorow 1974; Gilligan 1982; Jordan et al. 1991; Miller 1976.

22. Jordan et al. 1991.

23. For an overview of traditional adult development theories, see Kegan 1994.

24. For an overview of the way in which these internal and external forces are conceptualized and their relationship explored, see Brown and Gilligan 1992; Gilligan 1982; West and Zimmerman 1991.

25. Miller and Stiver 1997, p. 30.

26. Mary Parker Follett was an early advocate of the idea that a concept of "power with," based on principles of mutuality, might be linked to organizational effectiveness. Writing in the early 1920s, she proposed new models of organizational effectiveness that were based on principles of integration, power with, and something she called circular response. It is interesting, but not surprising, to note that many of her ideas were taken up by other (male) organizational theorists, but with these aspects of mutuality—and their challenge to hierarchical systems of power—silenced. For those interested in a firsthand account of her ideas, see Follett 1924. Those interested in current commentary on the way her ideas have been absent from or distorted in organizational theory, see Graham 1996.

27. See DeVault 1990 for a description of the work entailed in feeding a family and Ruddick 1989 for a description of maternal practice.

28. For a detailed description of the medical provider/client relationship, see Jacques 1992; Jordan et al. 1991; Parker 1997.

Chapter 3

1. In addition to the author, the seven-member research team for the overall project included Lotte Bailyn, Deborah Kolb, Susan Eaton, Maureen Harvey, Robin

Johnson, and Leslie Perlow. For an overview of the findings, please see Bailyn et al. 1996.

2. Morgan 1983.

3. For a description of the theory of culture that underlies ethnographic inquiry, see Spradley 1979. For examples of how this theory of culture has been applied to organizational studies, see Schein 1985 and Smircich 1983.

4. See Smith 1990, pp. 11–12, for a more detailed description of the term "line of fault." Readers interested in understanding more about how everyday actions reflect the ideology of the dominant power structures will find this book informative as well as easy to read. Smith captures the principle simply, without resorting to the complicated language often used by poststructuralists to describe the same idea.

5. For a detailed description of the methodology Jacques used in his study of nursing work, including an example of the logs, see Jacques 1992. For an overview of the theoretical roots of the practice of deconstructing social practice as text, see Jacobsen and Jacques 1997, pp. 48–49. For a description of how these data fit within a genealogical analysis of the social construction of the subject position "employee," see Jacques 1996.

6. The Ethnograph is available from Qualis Research Associates, P.O. Box 2240, Corvallis, OR 97339.

7. Some might say that my method of analysis differed from that described by Glaser and Strauss (1967) because I had explicitly identified some preliminary categories. In their view, a pure grounded theory approach begins with a blank slate and allows the categories to emerge from the data. In my opinion this is one of those research principles that is stated as an ideal but ignores the standpoint of the researcher. No one starts with a blank slate. All of us have a wealth of experience, values, and old frameworks that influence what "emerges" from the data. I made my preliminary categories explicit because I wanted to acknowledge the relational standpoint from which I intended to analyze the data.

8. The intrinsically iterative, emergent process of research analysis is rarely discussed in the methodological recounting of research findings. Most research reports ignore or obscure the inner workings of the research process and present it as far more linear and straightforward than was actually experienced by the researcher. For readers interested in understanding this process and analytic strategies to enhance it, I recommend Bailyn 1977. In this article Bailyn helps researchers to understand the interplay between concepts and data and what she calls the "cognitive flow" through which researchers develop conceptual grasp as the study progresses and how, as data emerge, they are integrally involved in the conceptualization process itself. Most important, she helps researchers to understand how being self-conscious about this process can add to the texture and usefulness of research findings.

9. See Jordan et al. 1991, p. 3.

10. For a description of the way all bureaucratic organizations exemplify stereotypically masculine values, see Acker 1990 and Ferguson 1984. For a description of the masculine nature of engineering work cultures in particular, see McIlwee and Robinson 1992.

11. For a more detailed description of the method and findings in the cultural diagnosis process, see Bailyn et al. 1996 and Perlow 1997. For a description of the techniques used in the diagnosis, see Levinson, Molinari, and Spohn 1972 and Schein 1985.

Chapter 4

1. Chapter 3 details the process of creating these criteria, i.e., the "relational lens" through which I viewed data. Briefly, I started with general criteria gleaned from relational principles (Jordan et al. 1991) and included new criteria as they emerged from the data. The decision about which behaviors qualified was subjective but not arbitrary. A description of the observed action and the rationale for its inclusion as "relational" is included with each example.

2. Unless otherwise noted, all quotes are from the six female engineers who participated in the study.

3. See Ruddick 1989.

4. For an example of the way in which empowerment is treated in the management literature, see Senge 1990.

5. Cato Wadel notes that outcomes embedded in people and in social interactions are invisible because they do not fit conventional definitions of outcomes. For a description of several other hidden aspects of everyday life, including the invisible work of being a good citizen, see Wadel 1979.

6. For a more detailed description of what is meant by the term "interacting sense of self," see Jordan et al. 1991 and Miller 1976.

7. Brown and Gilligan 1992.

8. For a fuller explanation of theories of experiential learning, see Kolb 1984 and Schon 1983.

9. See Held 1990.

10. For a description of the way in which this urgency plays itself out—sometimes with dysfunctional results—in relational interactions, particularly when there are status or power differences between the parties involved, see Brown and Gilligan 1992 and Jordan et al. 1991.

11. See Fishman 1978.

12. Miller and Stiver 1997, p. 30.

13. Miller 1986b.

14. Sara Ruddick's description of how mothers balance the competing demands of developing individuality and communal responsibility in children can be found

in Ruddick 1989. Marjorie DeVault's depiction of the work entailed in creating a sense of family through balancing individual and communal needs in providing a family meal can be found in DeVault 1990. These two analyses are focused on the behavioral manifestations of resolving the tension between individual and collective needs. For psychologically oriented analyses of the tension itself and its origins in early life experience, see Gillette 1990; McCollom 1990; Smith and Berg 1987.

15. Stiver 1991.

16. See Jacques 1992, p. 98.

Chapter 5

1. Our method of conducting a cultural diagnosis entailed gathering organizational narratives in response to questions about the definition of success, the attributes of the ideal engineer, and the perception about what types of behaviors were likely to lead to promotions.

2. For a general description of engineering environments, see McIlwee and Robinson 1992.

3. See McIlwee and Robinson 1992, p. 21.

4. In the late 1970s, there were many popular self-help books for women aspiring to make it into managerial ranks in business. The two most influential were Margaret Hennig and Ann Jardim's *The Managerial Woman* (1978) and Betty Harragan's *Games Mother Never Taught You* (1977). While relational practice offers an alternative interpretation of the behavior women were cautioned against in these books, I do not mean to imply that the books were not useful or informative. Like Deborah Tannen's *You Just Don't Understand* (1990), these books provide a useful description of stereotypically masculine behavior, values, and attributes. However, they do not question the privileging of these masculine norms or suggest that they might be problematic for business. The point of exploring relational practice is to do just that. It is offered as a way of exploring the possibility that privileging these masculine norms, interaction styles, and beliefs about routes to success unnecessarily constrain an organization's ability to think creatively and adapt to the needs of a changing world.

5. For an example of other ways in which women are treated as wives and mothers in organizations, see Huff 1990 and Kolb 1992.

6. This is not to suggest that there is no pathological expression of a relational model of growth-in-connection. Just as there are pathological expressions of individuation and autonomy, there are individuals who are too dependent on connection. Rather, the suggestion made here is that evidence of privileging the relational is *assumed,* in the dominant discourse, to indicate an abnormal rather than a normal state and this results in a commonsense understanding of it is as some form of aberration—pathology, dependency, or powerlessness—rather than as evidence of mental health.

Chapter 6

1. Hammer and Champy 1993, p. 71.

2. The business section of any popular bookstore contains a number of different books on the subject, each offering a slightly different perspective on the problem. How-to books and training programs for managers and leaders have proliferated. For a sampling of this extensive literature, see Bradford and Cohen 1998; Conger, Spreitzer, and Lawler 1999; Goleman 1998.

3. Senge 1990, p. 8.

4. Bradford and Cohen 1998, p. xvi.

5. Again, the literature is extensive. For a sampling, see Bass 1998; Heifetz 1994; Kotter 1996; Kouzes and Posner 1995.

6. Helgesen 1990; Rosener 1995.

7. Valian 1998, p. 7.

8. See Bailyn et al. (forthcoming).

9. See Morrison et al. 1987.

10. For studies with data collected primarily from white middle class women, see Ballard 1998; Marshall 1995; Moore and Buttner 1997. One of my colleagues at the Center for Gender in Organizations at Simmons Graduate School of Management, Deborah Meyerson, is in the process of analyzing interview data from a more diverse group of women and is finding similar results. Findings from these interviews will be published by Harvard University Press in a book tentatively entitled *Tempered Radicalism: Everyday Leadership Transforming Organizations*.

11. See Meyerson and Scully 1995.

12. See Weick 1984.

13. Kathy Kram, whose work is central to current conceptualizations of mentoring in organizations, recently has written about the mutuality involved in mentoring relationships. See, for example, Kram 1996.

14. Maureen Harvey, personal communication.

15. This is an important point that needs further development. It highlights one of the key dilemmas in espousing a relational model of effectiveness for organizations. The models of relational interactions we rely on to understand the principles of connection are drawn from relationships that are, more often than not, characterized by patriarchy or other unequal power relationships. In "What's Love Got to Do with It?" I begin to articulate the different dimensions of this issue. A copy of the working paper is available through the Center for Gender in Organizations, Simmons Graduate School of Management, 409 Commonwealth Avenue, Boston, MA 02215.

16. See Kolb and Williams (forthcoming).

17. See Kaplan et al. 1991.

18. See Kofodimus 1993.

19. See Covey 1990 and Goleman 1995; 1998.

20. For a more detailed description and typology of the ways organizations use gender as a resource, see Acker 1990.

21. Pierce 1996.

22. See, for example, Huff 1990; Jacques 1992; Kolb 1992; Parker 1997.

23. Harvey 1993.

24. See, for example, Benner et al. 1996; DeVault 1990; Ruddick 1989.

25. See Johansson 1995.

26. Miller 1986a, p. 40.

27. For additional readings on how uncommon and unexpected it is to connect these two spheres, see Fletcher and Bailyn 1996 and Bailyn, Fletcher, and Kolb 1997. Although linking the two spheres as a source of skills development is not addressed in these articles per se, they make the point that the separation is dysfunctional at many levels.

28. Many men do not fit ideal images of masculinity but feel obligated to fulfill them or disappear the ways they do not. One of the themes in the aforementioned Ford Foundation study of gender equity and work and personal life integration was the way men felt that their societal roles as breadwinners meant they must sacrifice everyday involvement in family and community in order to be "good" fathers and husbands. For a description and discussion of this theme, see Bailyn, Rapoport, and Fletcher (forthcoming).

29. Parker 1997.

30. For current descriptions of these concepts, see House and Aditya 1997; Lipnack and Stamps 1993; Seely Brown and Durguid 1991; Slater 1994.

31. Although there is a growing interest in organizational theory on the effect of negative relationships at work, the literature on this topic is limited. For a sampling of recent work in this area, see Dutton et al. 1998 and Labianca et al. 1998.

32. Morrison et al. 1987.

References

Acker, J. 1989. *Doing Comparable Worth: Gender, Class, and Pay Equity*. Philadelphia: Temple University Press.

———. 1990. "Hierarchies, Jobs, Bodies: A Theory of Gendered Organizations." *Gender and Society* 4: 139–158.

Alvesson, M., and S. Deetz. 1996. "Critical Theory and Postmodernist Approaches to Organizational Studies." In *Handbook of Organization Studies*, edited by S. Clegg, C. Hardy, and W. Nord (pp. 191–217). London: Sage.

Bailyn, L. 1993. *Breaking the Mold: Women, Men and Time in the New Corporate World*. New York: The Free Press.

———. 1977. "Research as a Cognitive Process: Implications for Data Analysis." *Quality and Quantity* 11: 97–117.

Bailyn, L., J. K. Fletcher, and D. Kolb. 1997. "Unexpected Connections: Considering Employees' Personal Lives Can Revitalize Your Business." *Sloan Management Review* 38 (4): 11–19.

Bailyn, L., R. Rapoport, and J. K. Fletcher (forthcoming). "Moving Organizations Toward Gender Equity: A Cautionary Tale." In *Organizational Change and Gender Equity: International Perspectives on Fathers and Mothers at the Workplace*, edited by Linda Haas. Newbury Park, Calif.: Sage.

Bailyn, L., R. Rapaport, D. Kolb, and J. K. Fletcher. 1996. "Re-linking Work and Family: A Catalyst for Organizational Change." Working Paper #3892-96. Cambridge, Mass.: MIT Sloan School of Management.

Ballard, N. 1998. "The Stalactite Palace." Working Report. Wellesley, Mass.: Wellesley College Center for Research on Women.

Bass, B. 1998. *Transformational Leadership*. Mahwah, N.J.: Lawrence Erlbaum.

Bellah, R., R. Madsen, W. Sullivan, A. Swidler, and S. Tipton. 1985. *Habits of the Heart*. Berkeley: University of California Press.

Benner, P., C. A. Tanner, and C. A. Chesla. 1996. *Expertise in Nursing Practice*. New York: Springer.

Benner, P., and J. Wrubel. 1989. *The Primacy of Caring*. Menlo Park, Calif.: Addison-Wesley.

Bradford, D., and A. Cohen. 1998. *Power Up*. New York: John Wiley and Sons.

Bradley, H. 1993. "Across the Great Divide." In *Doing Women's Work*, edited by C. L. Williams (pp. 10–27). London: Sage.

———. 1989. *Men's Work, Women's Work*. Minneapolis: University of Minnesota Press.

Brown, L. M., and C. Gilligan. 1992. *Meeting at the Crossroads*. Boston: Harvard University Press.

Calás, M. B., and L. Smircich. 1993. "Dangerous Liaisons: The 'Feminine-in-Management' meets 'Globalization.'" *Business Horizons* (March/April): 73–83.

Calás, M. B., and L. Smircich. 1996. "From the Women's Point of View: Feminist Approaches to Organization Studies." In *Handbook of Organization Studies*, edited by S. Clegg, W. Nord, and C. Hardy (pp. 218–259). London: Sage.

———. 1991. "Using the 'F' Word: Feminist Theories and the Social Consequences of Organizational Research." In *Gendering Organizational Analysis*, edited by A. J. Mills and P. Tancred (pp. 222–234). London: Sage.

Calvert, L., and V. J. Ramsey. 1992. "Bringing Women's Voice to Research on Women in Management: A Feminist Perspective." *Journal of Management Inquiry* 1 (1): 79–88.

Child, J. 1996. "Follett: Constructive Conflict." In *Mary Parker Follett: Prophet of Management*, edited by P. Graham. Cambridge, Mass.: Harvard Business School Press.

Chodorow, N. 1974. "Family Structure and Feminine Personality." In *Women, Culture, and Society*, edited by M. Z. Rosaldo and L. Lamphere (pp. 44–64). Stanford, Calif.: Stanford University Press.

Clegg, S. 1989. *Frameworks of Power*. Newbury Park, Calif.: Sage.

Cockburn, C. 1991. *In the Way of Women: Men's Resistance to Sex Equality in Organizations*. Ithaca, N.Y.: ILR Press.

Collinson, D. 1994. "Strategies of Resistance: Power, Knowledge, and Subjectivity in the Workplace." In *Resistance and Power in Organizations*, edited by J. M. Jermier, D. Knights, and W. Nord (pp. 25–69). London: Routledge.

Collinson, D., and J. Hearn. 1994. "Naming Men as Men: Implications for Work, Organization, and Management." *Gender, Work and Organization* 1 (1): 2–22.

Conger, J., G. Spreitzer, and E. Lawler. 1999. *Leader's Change Handbook*. San Francisco: Jossey-Bass.

Connell, R. W. 1995. *Masculinities*. Berkeley: University of California Press.

Covey, S. 1990. *The Seven Habits of Highly Effective People*. New York: Simon and Schuster.

Daniels, A. K. 1987. "Invisible Work." *Social Problems* 34 (5): 403–415.

DeVault, M. 1990. *Feeding the Family*. Chicago: University of Chicago Press.

Diamond, I., and L. Quinby. 1988. *Feminism and Foucault*. Boston: Northeastern University Press.

Drucker, P. 1996. "Mary Parker Follett: Prophet of Management." In *Mary Parker Follett: Prophet of Management,* edited by P. Graham (pp. 1–11). Cambridge, Mass.: Harvard Business School Press.

Dutton, J., G. Debebe, and A. Drzesniewski. 1998. "Being Valued and Devalued at Work." Working paper. Ann Arbor: School of Management, University of Michigan.

Ewick, P., and S. Silbey. 1995. "Subversive Stories and Hegemonic Tales: Toward a Sociology of Narrative." *Law and Society Review* 29 (2): 197–226.

Fairclough, N. 1989. *Language and Power.* New York: Longman.

Ferguson, K. E. 1984. *The Feminist Case against Bureaucracy.* Philadelphia: Temple University Press.

Fierman, J. 1990. "Do Women Manage Differently?" *Fortune* (Dec. 17): 115–118.

Fineman, S. 1993. "Organizations as Emotional Arenas." In *Emotion in Organizations,* edited by S. Fineman (pp. 9–35). London: Sage.

Fishman, P. 1978. "Interaction: The Work Women Do." *Social Problems* 25: 397–406.

Flax, J. 1990. *Thinking Fragments.* Berkeley: University of California Press.

Fletcher, J. K. 1994. "Castrating the Female Advantage: Feminist Standpoint Research and Management Science." *Journal of Management Inquiry* 3 (1): 74–82.

———. 1998. "What's Love Got to Do with It?" *CGO Working Paper Series,* no. 4. Boston: Center for Gender in Organizations, Simmons Graduate School of Management.

Fletcher, J. K., and L. Bailyn. 1996. "Challenging the Last Boundary." In *The Boundaryless Career,* edited by M. Arthur and D. Rousseau (pp. 256–267). Oxford: Oxford University Press.

Follett, M. P. 1924. *Creative Experience.* New York: Longmans Green.

Foucault, M. 1980. "Truth and Power." In *Power/Knowledge: Selected Interviews and Other Writings, 1972–1977, by Michel Foucault,* edited by C. Gordon (pp. 109–133). New York: Pantheon.

Friedlander, F. 1994. "Toward Whole Systems and Whole People." *Organization* 1: 59–64.

Game, A., and R. Pringle. 1983. *Gender at Work.* Boston: George Allen & Unwin.

Gardner, H. 1993. *Multiple Intelligences: The Theory in Practice.* New York: Basic Books.

Gherardi, S. 1995. *Gender, Symbolism, and Organizational Cultures.* London: Sage.

Gillette, J. 1990. "Intimacy in Work Groups: Looking from the Inside Out." In *Groups in Context,* edited by J. Gillette and M. McCollom. Reading, Mass.: Addison Wesley.

Gilligan, C. 1982. *In a Different Voice.* Cambridge, Mass.: Harvard University Press.

Glaser, B., and A. Strauss. 1967. *The Discovery of Grounded Theory: Strategies and Qualitative Research.* Hawthorne, New York: Aldine de Gruyter.

Goleman, D. 1995. *Emotional Intelligence.* New York: Bantam Books.

———. 1998. *Working with Emotional Intelligence.* New York: Bantam Books.

Graham, P. (ed.). 1996. *Mary Parker Follett: Prophet of Management.* Cambridge, Mass.: Harvard Business School Press.

Grant, J. 1988. "Women as Managers: What They Can Offer to Organizations." *Organizational Dynamics* (Spring): 56–63.

Hammer, M., and J. Champy. 1993. *Re-engineering the Corporation.* New York: Harper Collins.

Harding, S. 1987. *Feminism and Methodology.* Bloomington: Indiana University Press.

———. 1986. *The Science Question in Feminism.* Ithaca, N.Y.: Cornell University Press.

Harragan, B. 1977. *Games Mother Never Taught You.* New York: Warner Books.

Hartmann, H. 1983. "Capitalism, Patriarchy, and Job Segregation by Sex." In *The Signs Reader,* edited by E. Abel and E. Abel. Chicago: University of Chicago Press.

Harvey, M. 1993. "The Stone Center Project at DEC." Unpublished report. Wellesley, Mass.: The Stone Center, Wellesley College.

Heifetz, R. 1994. *Leadership without Easy Answers.* Cambridge, Mass.: Harvard University Press.

Held, V. 1990. "Mothering vs. Contract." In *Beyond Self-Interest,* edited by Jane Mansbridge (pp. 287–347). Chicago: University of Chicago Press.

Helgesen, S. 1990. *The Female Advantage: Women's Ways of Leadership.* New York: Doubleday.

Hennig, M., and A. Jardim. 1978. The Managerial Woman. New York: Pocket Books.

House, R. J., and R. Aditya. 1997. "The Social Scientific Study of Leadership: Quo Vadis?" *Journal of Management* 23 (3): 409–473.

Huff, A. 1990. "Wives—of the Organization." Paper presented at the Women and Work Conference, Arlington, Texas, May.

Jacobsen, S., and R. Jacques. 1989. "Beyond Androgyny: Future Directions for Gender Research." Paper presented at the Academy of Management Meeting, Washington, D.C., August.

———. 1997. "Destabilizing the Field." *Journal of Management Inquiry* 6 (1): 42–59.

Jacques, R. 1996. *Manufacturing the Employee: Management Knowledge from the 19th to 21st Centuries.* London: Sage.

———. 1992. "Re-presenting the Knowledge Worker: A Poststructuralist Analysis of the New Employed Professional." Unpublished doctoral dissertation. Amherst: University of Massachusetts.

Jaques, E. 1979. "Taking Time Seriously." *Harvard Business Review* (Sept.–Oct.): 124–132.

Johansson, U. 1995. "*Constructing the Responsible Worker: Changing Structures, Changing Selves.*" Paper presented at the Academy of Management Meeting, Vancouver, B.C., August.

Jordan, J., A. Kaplan, J. B. Miller, I. Stiver, and J. Surrey. 1991. *Women's Growth in Connection.* New York: The Guilford Press.

Kanter, R. 1977. *Men and Women of the Corporation.* New York: Basic Books.

Kanter, Rosabeth Moss. 1996. "Preface." In *Mary Parker Follett: Prophet of Management,* edited by P. Graham (pp. xiii–xix). Cambridge, Mass.: Harvard Business School Press.

Kaplan, R., W. Drath, and J. Kofodimos. 1991. *Beyond Ambition.* San Francisco: Jossey-Bass.

Kegan, R. 1994. *In Over Our Heads.* Cambridge, Mass.: Harvard University Press.

Kofodimos, J. 1993. *Balancing Act.* San Francisco: Jossey-Bass.

Kolb, D. A. 1984. *Experiential Learning.* Englewood Cliffs, N.J.: Prentice-Hall.

Kolb, D. M. 1992. "Women's Work: Peacemaking in Organizations." In *Hidden Conflict in Organizations: Uncovering Behind the Scenes Disputes,* edited by D. M. Kolb and J. M. Bartunek (pp. 63–91). Newbury Park, Calif.: Sage.

Kolb, D., and J. Williams. (forthcoming). *Tough Enough.* New York: Simon and Schuster.

Kotter, J. 1996. *Leading Change.* Cambridge: Harvard Business School Press.

Kouzes, J., and B. Posner. 1995. *The Leadership Challenge.* San Francisco: Jossey-Bass.

Kram, K. 1996. "A Relational Approach to Career Development." In *The Career Is Dead: Long Live the Career,* edited by D. T. Hall (pp. 132–157). San Francisco: Jossey-Bass.

Labianca, G., D. Brass, and B. Gray. 1998. "Social Networks and Perceptions of Intergroup Conflict: The Role of Negative Relationships and Third Parties." *Academy of Management Journal* 41 (1): 55–67.

Levinson, H., J. Molinari, and A. Spohn. 1972. *Organizational Diagnosis.* Cambridge, Mass.: Harvard University Press.

Lipnack, J., and J. Stamps. 1993. *The TeamNet Factor: Bringing the Power of Boundary-Crossing into the Heart of Your Business.* New York: Wiley.

Lorber, J. 1991. "Dismantling Noah's Ark." In *The Social Construction of Gender,* edited by J. Lorber and S. Farrell (pp. 355–370). Newbury Park: Sage.

Lukes, S. 1974. *Power.* London: Macmillan.

March, J. and H. Simon. 1958. *Organizations.* New York: John Wiley and Sons.

March, J. G., and J. P. Olsen. 1976. *Ambiguity and Choice in Organizations.* Oslo: Universitetsforlaget.

Marshall, J. 1995. *Women Managers Moving On: Exploring Career and Life Choices.* London: Routledge.

Martin, J., and Knopoff, K. 1995. "The Gendered Implications of Apparently Gender-Neutral Theory: Re-reading Weber." In *Ruffin Lecture Series Vol. 3: Business Ethics and Women's Studies.* edited by E. Freeman and A. Larson. Oxford, England: Oxford University Press.

Martin, P. Y. 1995. "Mobilized Masculinities and Glass Ceilings." Paper presented at the Academy of Management Meeting. Vancouver, B.C., August.

McCollom, M. 1990. "Group Formation: Boundaries, Leadership, and Culture." In *Groups in Context,* edited by J. Gillette and M. McCollom. Reading, Mass.: Addison Wesley.

McIlwee, J., and J. G. Robinson. 1992. *Women in Engineering.* Albany: SUNY Press.

Meyerson, D. (forthcoming) *Tempered Radicalism: Everyday Leadership Transforming Organizations.* Cambridge, Mass.: Harvard University Press.

Meyerson, D., and M. Scully. 1995. "Tempered Radicalism and the Politics of Ambivalence and Change." *Organization Science* 6 (5): 585–600.

Miller, J. B. 1976. *Toward a New Psychology of Women.* Boston: Beacon Press.

———. 1986a. *Toward a New Psychology of Women.* 2d ed. Boston: Beacon Press.

———. 1986b. "What Do We Mean by Relationships?" *Work in Progress Series,* no. 22. Wellesley, Mass.: The Stone Center, Wellesley College.

Miller, J. B., and I. Stiver. 1997. *The Healing Connection.* Boston: Beacon Press.

Mills, A. J., and P. Tancred. 1992. "Introduction." In *Gendering Organizational Analysis,* edited by A. J. Mills and P. Tancred (pp. 1–8). Newbury Park, Calif.: Sage.

Mintzberg, H. 1973. *The Nature of Managerial Work.* Englewood Cliffs, N.J.: Prentice-Hall.

Moore, D. P., and E. H. Buttner. 1997. *Women Entrepreneurs: Moving beyond the Glass Ceiling.* London: Sage.

Morgan, G. 1983. "Research Strategies: Modes of Engagement." In *Beyond Method,* edited by Gareth Morgan. Newbury Park, Calif.: Sage.

Morrison, A., R. White, and E. Van Velsor. 1987. *Breaking the Glass Ceiling.* Reading, Mass.: Addison-Wesley.

Mumby, D. K. 1988. *Communication and Power in Organizations: Discourse, Ideology, and Domination.* Norwood, N.J.: Ablex.

Mumby, D. K., and L. Putnam. 1992. "The Politics of Emotion: A Feminist Reading of Bounded Rationality." *Academy of Management Review* 17 (3): 465–486.

Parker, V. 1997. "Relational Work in Organizational Contexts." Unpublished doctoral dissertation. Boston: Boston University.

Parkin, W. 1993. "The Public and the Private: Gender, Sexuality, and Emotion." In *Emotion in Organizations,* edited by S. Fineman (pp. 167–189). London: Sage.

Parsons, T., and R. F. Bales. 1955. *Family, Socialization, and Interaction Process.* New York: The Free Press.

Perlow, L. 1997. *Finding Time.* Ithaca, N.Y.: Cornell University Press.

Perrow, C. 1986. *Complex Organizations.* 3d ed. New York: Random House.

Pierce, J. 1996. *Gender Trials: Emotional Lives in Contemporary Law Firms.* Los Angeles: University of California Press.

Reverby, S. 1987. *Ordered to Care: The Dilemma of American Nursing, 1850–1945.* Cambridge: Cambridge University Press.

Roberts, J. 1990. "Uncovering Hidden Caring." *Nursing Outlook* 38 (2): 67–69.

Rosener, J. 1995. *America's Competitive Secret: Women Managers.* New York: Oxford University Press.

———. 1990. "Ways Women Lead." *Harvard Business Review,* (Nov.–Dec.): 119–125.

Ruddick, S. 1989. *Maternal Thinking.* Boston: Beacon Press.

Schein, E. 1985. *Organizational Culture and Leadership.* San Francisco, Calif.: Jossey-Bass.

Schon, D. 1983. *The Reflective Practitioner.* New York: Basic Books.

Seely Brown, J., and P. Durguid. 1991. "Organizational Learning and Communities-of-Practice: Toward a Unified View of Working, Learning, and Innovation." *Organization Science* 2 (1): 40–57.

Senge, P. 1990. *The Fifth Discipline.* New York: Doubleday.

Slater, R. 1994. *Get Better or Get Beaten? 31 Leadership Secrets from Jack Welch.* Burr Ridge, IL: Richard D. Irwin.

Smircich, L. 1983. "Concepts of Culture and Organizational Analysis." *Administrative Science Quarterly* 28: 339–358.

———. 1985. "Toward a Woman-Centered Organization Theory." Paper presented at the Academy of Management Annual Meeting, San Diego, Calif., August.

Smith, D. 1990. *The Conceptual Practices of Power.* Boston: Northeastern University Press.

Smith, K., and D. Berg. 1987. *Paradoxes of Group Life.* San Francisco: Jossey-Bass.

Spradley, J. 1979. *The Ethnographic Interview.* New York: Holt, Rinehart and Winston.

Sternberg, R. J. 1985. *Beyond I.Q.* New York: Cambridge University Press.

Stiver, I. 1991. "The Meanings of Dependency in Female–Male Relationships." In *Women's Growth in Connection,* edited by J. Jordan, A. Kaplan, J. B. Miller, I. Stiver, and J. Surrey. New York: The Guilford Press.

Tannen, D. 1990. *You Just Don't Understand.* New York: Morrow.

Taylor, F. 1911. *The Principles of Scientific Management.* New York: Norton.

Valian, V. 1998. *Why So Slow? The Advancement of Women.* Cambridge, Mass.: MIT Press.

Vroom, V. H. 1973. "A New Look at Managerial Decision Making." *Organizational Dynamics* 1(4): 66–80.

Vroom, V., and P. Yetten. 1973. *Leadership and Decision Making.* Pittsburgh: University of Pittsburgh Press.

Wadel, C. 1979. "The Hidden Work of Everyday Life." In *The Social Anthropology of Work,* edited by S. Wallman (pp. 365–384). New York: Academic Press.

Weber, M. 1964. *The Theory of Social and Economic Organizations.* New York: Free Press of Glencoe.

Weedon, C. 1987. *Feminist Practice and Poststructuralist Theory.* Oxford: Basil Blackwell.

Weick, K. 1984. "Small Wins: Redefining the Scale of Social Problems." *American Psychologist* 39 (1): 40–49.

West, C., and D. Zimmerman. 1991. "Doing Gender." In *The Social Construction of Gender,* edited by J. Lorber and S. Farrell (pp. 13–37). Newbury Park, Calif.: Sage.

Index